Start Your Own
CHILDCARE
Business

Johannesburg • Oxford
San Diego • Sydney • Toronto

This book was developed in association with the National Business Library.

Editor: Dawn Kilgore
Production Editor: Dawn Kilgore
Interior Designer: Nicola Ruskin
Page Compositor: Judy Whalen
Cover: Tom Lewis, Inc.

Pfeiffer & Company
8517 Production Avenue
San Diego, CA 92121-2280
Editorial Offices: (619) 578-5900, FAX (619) 578-2042
Orders: (606) 647-3030, FAX (606) 647-3034

Library of Congress Cataloging-in-Publication Data

Start your own childcare business.
     p/ cm. — (Start your own)
  Includes index.
  ISBN 0-89384-287-7 (pbk.)
  1. Child care centers—United States—Handbooks, manuals, etc.
2. Day care centers—United States—Handbooks, manuals, etc. 3. New
business enterprises—United States—Handbooks, manuals, etc.
I. Series.
HQ778.63.S73   1995
362.7'12–dc20   95-33974
                                                      CIP

Printed in the United States of America.

Printing 1 2 3 4 5 6 7 8 9 10

CONTENTS

PREFACE

Start Your Own Childcare Business is the result of many hours of in-depth research into the childcare industry. Our exclusive team of National Business Library's professional business writers and Pfeiffer & Company's professional editors has brought years of practical experience to this project, and we know that the information provided in this book will set you on the road to success.

Owning your own business can be the most exciting and rewarding venture you will ever experience. We talk to hundreds of small business owners who make comments like, "Doing something I really enjoy makes every new day a pleasure," or "If I had known I could be realizing this kind of income, rather than making my former boss wealthy, I would have started my own business years ago."

It's true! You'll never get rich working for someone else. By capitalizing on your experience, investing time and energy, and studying the proven techniques and business methods provided in this book, you will be well on the way to realizing your goals for success in your own venture. It takes courage to begin. Without a doubt, the first step is the hardest—and you have already taken it!

INTRODUCTION:
A CRYING NEED FOR CHILDCARE

Ask any parent to name their primary concerns about raising children and chances are that, following good health and safety, they will mention quality childcare. Being able to find someone caring and reliable to leave our children with while we are working or busy is an age-old problem.

Never before have we seen such incredible numbers of mothers in the work force. The U. S. Census Bureau indicates that there are close to 40 million working women in America. These women have approximately 10 million children under six years old who require childcare. It is estimated that by 1995, the number of preschool children with working mothers will reach an astonishing 14.5 million!

Your decision to start your own childcare center and capitalize on the growing need in this country is one that will guarantee profits. The advantages of the business are that you do not need a degree, it can be started with minimum capital in your home before branching out into a commercial location and, according to those owner/operators we interviewed, it has a very high satisfaction ratio.

The profit potential ranges from $12,000 to $20,000 per year for a small home-based operation all the way up to $750,000 or more, as is the case with commercial-based operations having several locations in a densely populated area. In the latter case, the largest percentage of your expenses will be allocated to cover the salaries of experienced caregivers; a most important feature in attracting a steady clientele.

Before embarking on the road to starting your childcare center, there are several decisions you must make

♦ Do you genuinely enjoy working with children enough to consider making it a full-time venture?

♦ Are you able to develop creative programs that will keep active little minds and bodies occupied, safe and happy?

♦ Is your interest more geared to working with infants, toddlers between the ages of one and three, or youngsters of three to five years old?

♦ Are you willing to undertake the administrative aspects of running the business?

Even if you answered "no" to any of these questions, there is still tremendous potential for you in this business. If working with children is not your strong point, you can make a handsome profit by hiring people who do have the required child development skills.

If, on the other hand, you prefer to devote your attention to your love and affinity for children, you can easily make arrangements to have someone else handle the paperwork.

The information provided in this book will help you find your way through the start-up process. It will give you insights on how to structure your childcare business, additional services to offer parents and their children, how to establish a fee structure, and the best ways to promote your business.

The future for childcare services is guaranteed. The number of working mothers and single-parent families continues to grow and birth rates are expected to remain at an average of 3.5 million new babies per year through the end of the Twentieth Century! The time is ripe to secure your place in this booming market.

1

THE GROWTH OF
SMALL BUSINESS

The 1980s were referred to as America's "entrepreneurial era."
In 1986, more than 750,000 new businesses were created in the
United States. In 1989, more than a million new ventures were
started nationwide—almost half of them by women. In 1991, there
were 20.5 million small businesses in the United States—and the
entrepreneurial era is continuing through the 1990s. The recession
of the early 1990s compelled suddenly unemployed people to start
their own businesses in order to survive. An upsurge in part-time
businesses has also fueled an entrepreneurial trend, with people
in search of extra income working on profitable ventures during
their off-hours.

More and more people are opting to leave their 9-to-5 jobs
and stop "making someone else rich" to focus their energies on
building a successful business of their own. The combined circumstances of fewer advancement opportunities, lack of job security,
and the possibility of retiring without a pension are also driving
the trend toward self-employment.

Today, the number of individuals who are self-employed is at
its highest level ever, and based on your interest in this book, it's

quite possible that you'll be joining the ranks of small business owners in the near future. It may be simply a dream right now, but that's how these businesses start.

> *You can never be too young, too old, too busy, or too poor to start a business.*

Starting and operating your own small business is one of the most exciting and satisfying challenges you can undertake. There are no limitations on income potential when you're investing time and energy in your own enterprise. With the practical information provided in this book and dedication to your business goals, your chances for success are excellent.

What Is a Small Business?

The majority of businesses in the United States today are classified as small businesses. The definitions of what constitutes a small business run the gamut from the size of the overall staff (typically under 100) to the amount of assets or sales volume. However, in this book, small business is defined as one that is independently owned and operated.

The major benefit of this type of business is that you have the ability to make decisions quickly and act on them immediately. What typically bogs down big business is the number of people involved in the decision-making process.

Other advantages include the fact that small businesses can provide personalized service to the community or the market they're serving and the owner has the freedom, independence, and control to operate exactly as he or she chooses.

It's important to remember, however, that most major corporations, from Ford Motor Company and McDonald's to Mary Kay Cosmetics, started out as small businesses—as dreams.

It was because of basic business sense and a willingness to learn and adapt as their companies grew that Henry Ford, Ray Kroc, and Mary Kay, and thousands like them, steered their dreams into monumental financial successes.

Whether your goal is to supplement an existing income and to operate a solely owned home-based business from your garage, kitchen table, or spare bedroom, or to start a business that involves raising substantial capital, finding and setting up a commercial location, and hiring employees, you have the potential to enjoy an independent lifestyle that carries with it a number of rewards. And the rewards are as varied as the people who pursue them.

Accepting the Challenge

Remember, these rewards do not come without hard work and the willingness to research and understand all facets of running your business. Many new businesses fail within the first few years.

Reasons given for the early demise of a small business range from lack of organization or management experience to undercapitalization, misunderstanding of the importance of advertising, inexperience in pricing products and services, lack of an overall business plan, improper hiring practices, and failure to accurately assess the competition.

Entrepreneur
A person who undertakes an independent enterprise; one who has made the decision to go into business for him/herself.

It isn't that someone purposely starts a business without having explored these areas. However, many times a person feels that his or her demonstrated expertise while in the employ of another can easily be transferred into a personal business. This is only partially true.

While it is imperative that you have particular skills or talents—because selling them is what your ultimate success will be based on—it's equally important to understand how to sell them, to know exactly what your profit margin is, and what steps you need to take to ensure the continued growth of your business.

Sounds easy, right? It really can be. But like anything else worth doing, starting your own business means careful planning. For example, you wouldn't consider taking a month-long vacation without doing some serious planning to ensure that the house was taken care of while you were gone, that you had made reservations for lodging, tours, and flights, and that you had converted your cash into traveler's checks.

There are so many aspects involved in running a business, it is vital to be prepared for any eventuality. Being prepared means being informed, so that when situations do arise you know how to deal with them.

Is "Failure" Really Failure?

We have all heard stories about people who started their businesses on a shoestring and who became successful because of their sheer determination to make it work. It does happen, but these people are the exception rather than the rule, and in most cases have had experts standing behind them to give them guidance when problems came up. Others fail and, unfortunately, this often holds potential new business owners back. We hear and read about amazingly high figures related to so-called business failures.

According to a research project conducted by Albert Shapero, professor of the American Free Enterprise System at Ohio State University for many years, no one really knows the true failure rate of new businesses. The main reason for this is because there is not really a standard definition of "failure" in this case. He points out that a number of businesses close for a variety of reasons, many of which are not documented.

For example, in some cases the owners reach retirement age and have no one to pass the business along to; others shut down because the owners simply get bored; while still other entrepreneurs file a Chapter 11 bankruptcy, which basically gives them the opportunity to stay in business and continue operating under a court-approved plan, even though they become a statistic on the "failure" list.

The other extremely important aspect to consider when thinking about the benefits and risks of starting your own business is that having a business fail has never been a deterrent for true entrepreneurs. Many well-known business moguls failed at least once, and often more than once, before striking it rich.

Learning From Experience

In fact, almost anyone who has had a business fail will tell you that the experience was more valuable than anything they could have been taught in a business school, and that it provided them with the knowledge they needed to start another venture success-fully. This kind of determination is a valid qualification for self-employment and will pay off handsomely.

When you own your own business, you are responsible for everything. There will be times, such as when your accounts receivable are running sixty days late or the phone company puts the wrong number in your Yellow Pages listing, when returning to the 9-to-5 world will seem like a tempting option.

This is where self-discipline, an unwavering belief in your product or service, and the determination to be your own boss will pull you through.

But, again, we can't stress enough the importance of planning, understanding basic business practices, being aware of consumer trends, and taking the time to develop, implement, and update goals to ensure success for your efforts.

What This Book Offers

This book is designed to provide you with the information you will need to start your childcare business, to offer techniques to help you with day-to-day operations, and to provide anecdotes about people just like you who had a dream and, through planning and determination, were able to turn that dream into a successful reality.

In addition to focusing on aspects of the childcare business, we cover such important business matters as

- ◆ Recognizing the entrepreneurial profile
- ◆ Taking our exclusive Entrepreneurial Quiz
- ◆ Finding the right audience for your business through easy marketing techniques
- ◆ Organizing for efficiency
- ◆ Recognizing legalities

♦ Addressing financial concerns

♦ Getting your home office up and running

♦ Charting your enterprise's growth

You will find specific how-to information on

♦ Advertising and promoting your business

♦ Finding capital

♦ Saving money on operating expenses

♦ Developing a simple bookkeeping system that will show you whether you're facing a financial crisis or realizing a profit

You're never too young, too old, too busy, or too poor to start a business. Owning your own business means taking advantage of our marvelous system of free enterprise. Earning a substantial living and, even better, realizing a profit for doing something you enjoy is the American dream come true.

The road to financial independence through self-employment is challenging and rewarding.

The opportunities for entrepreneurs have never been better. Armed with a solid product or service to sell, the determination to succeed and, most important, business know-how, there is nothing that can stand in your way.

Notes

Key Points
_____
_____
_____
_____
_____
_____
_____

Personal Thoughts
_____
_____
_____
_____
_____
_____

Additional Research
_____
_____
_____
_____
_____
_____
_____

2

THE ENTREPRENEURIAL PROFILE

Starting a business is one thing, making it work is another. We know that success in self-employment is largely the result of careful planning and an understanding of basic business techniques and formulas.

As many successful entrepreneurs claim, making money doing something you love is the best way to ensure a profitable future. It is always easier to address the inevitable business challenges that crop up when you are creating a product or providing a service that gives you a sense of pleasure and personal satisfaction.

> *Start a business based on your expertise in a specific field and focus your involvement in an area that you thoroughly enjoy.*

Personality is a significant factor in determining what kind of business to get involved in, the way you will eventually set up the legal structure (sole proprietorship, partnership, etc.), and how you will run the business on a day-to-day basis. For example, if you are planning to start a business that is based on your artistic or creative abilities, it is possible that your personality is not suited to the very important aspect of sales. But without strong selling abilities, there is a likelihood that your goal of distributing, for example, your hand-carved wooden boxes nationally will not come to fruition.

This isn't to say that you should decide against going into business for yourself. It simply indicates that it would be in your best interest to join forces with someone who does have strong selling skills, who believes in the product as much as you do, and who will work with you toward a common goal.

On the other hand, if your personality is geared to working with people, it is a good idea to consider a business that will emphasize this ability, such as developing seminars or workshops based on your area of expertise, providing independent counseling or tutoring, or providing a service such as gift-basket designing or desktop publishing, which depends on your interaction with people on a one-to-one or a group basis for success.

Research shows that in order to address the many and varied situations that arise in business ownership, the true entrepreneur should possess the following personality traits.

Ten Important Entrepreneurial Traits

1. Self-awareness	6. Decisiveness
2. Self-motivation	7. Experience
3. Courage	8. Knowledge
4. Confidence	9. Perseverance
5. Patience	10. Drive

1. *Self-awareness.* Know who you are, what you're good at, and what you like to do. Start a business that is based on your expertise in a specific field and focus your involvement in an area that you thoroughly enjoy.

2. *Self-motivation.* Self-motivation is one of the most important personality traits of successful entrepreneurs. This is the characteristic that gets you going and keeps you moving when you are in business for yourself. It's what helps you to keep turning out those craft items, upgrading your technical skills, or developing new and improved promotional techniques when business is slow. It's what gives you the tenacity and confidence to call on a potential client even though you've heard "No" three times.

   Self-motivation is also what helps you overcome the fears and concerns that inevitably arise when you own your own business. It is the main ingredient that has spurred on people who have achieved success despite drawbacks, such as minimal capital, lack of education, or limited experience.

   People with a high degree of self-motivation see the greatest obstacles, such as learning a new aspect of business management, as a new and exciting challenge to overcome. If you've ever undertaken a project without fully understanding the mechanics involved in performing the task or knowing what the outcome would be, you were operating on self-motivation—the conviction that you would be able to learn whatever was needed to accomplish your goal.

   And regardless of the outcome of the project, you undoubtedly gained more experience and knowledge than you had before, which only works to increase your sense of motivation to handle new challenges.

3. *Courage.* Courage or the willingness to take risks is a valuable trait when striving for success. A successful person might say something like: "I don't know how I did it; I just made a phone call and asked for the money I needed." It was more than luck that made it possible for this person to raise the needed capital to get a business off the ground; it was the willingness to take a chance and hope for a positive response to the request.

The owner of a small cabinet-refinishing business said, "I always figure that the worst thing that can happen is someone will say no, so it never hurts to try." In the game of business, you must be willing to take chances. Even if you don't get exactly what you want every time, the odds are good that if you feel strongly about what you need, you will get it. But you have to ask!

4. **Confidence.** The age-old philosophy of positive thinking is a major step in the direction of success. By behaving as if you already are a success at what you do, it follows that you will be, and your customers will believe it, too. A confident attitude is one of the most appealing traits you can exhibit to prospective clients, for it lets them know that they will be getting the best their money can buy.

> *You have to accept whatever comes, and the important thing is that you meet it with courage and with the best you have to give.*
>
> Eleanor Roosevelt

5. **Patience.** When you own your own business, there will be times when you feel like the roof is caving in, especially when your suppliers seem to be taking their own sweet time in fulfilling an important order or when a customer's demands seem to be unrealistic. Although you may be able to hurry the supplier along, you must remember that your customers are always right, since they are the ones who will make or break your business.

If you are aware that patience is not your strong suit, develop a stop-gap exercise to use at times when coping is a definite necessity. Whether you count to ten before saying a word, visualize a pleasant scene, or repeat a secret phrase to yourself when tension is running high, it will be to your advantage.

6. **Decisiveness.** Business has been described as a process of making one fast decision after another. Often, a deci-

sion has to be made immediately, on the spur of the moment. In those instances, you should go with your intuition and trust that you are doing the right thing.

However, if you are the type of person who prefers to analyze your options, weigh all the factors, and make decisions slowly, then that is what you must do. It will keep your confidence intact and ensure that you're taking the right action. Again, careful planning will help you predict many of the decision-making situations that arise in your business. As time goes by and you grow more comfortable in your role as business owner, you will undoubtedly find yourself making quicker decisions.

7. *Experience.* A primary reason some businesses fail within a few years of start-up is lack of business experience. Whether or not your experience is directly related to the business you are planning to start, it is a key component for growth.

If you feel you do not have enough business experience, there are several avenues you can take before starting your own enterprise. Returning to school for specialized courses is one consideration. Most community colleges and adult education facilities offer classes and seminars in business start-up and maintenance, and there are hundreds of home-study or correspondence courses that will, in many cases, give you official certification in your field.

However, your best solution is to take a job in the field you're interested in. By asking questions about all the aspects of the business, you will gain experience, get paid for learning, and find out whether this is really what you want to do before sinking money, time, and energy into the enterprise.

8. *Knowledge.* Experience in your field is invaluable, but it is not enough. You have a better chance of succeeding the more you know about such vital factors as business basics, the product or service that you want to sell, the industry you are entering, your competition, and

the local, regional, state, and/or national markets. Do
your homework.

9. ***Perseverance.*** One of the adages you will hear time and
time again when talking to entrepreneurs is that perseverance is 90 percent of the battle to succeed.

   If you are like the majority of new small business
   owners, the entire staff and support system for your
   venture is probably *you.* Making a dream come true can
   be a lonely task, especially when you are just getting
   started, and ensuring that it works often means little rest
   or relaxation. You must be willing to persevere during the
   rough times, to hang in there during the slow periods,
   and to maintain your belief in your product or service—
   even when it seems like no one else in the world knows
   you exist. It has been written that through perseverance
   the snail reached the ark. So it is with success!

10. ***Drive.*** You must believe in your goal and be determined
    to succeed. The successful businessperson does not view
    obstacles or stumbling blocks as problems, but rather as
    challenges. To make your business a success, you need
    to be totally committed and willing to work long hours,
    especially in the beginning. If you do not have the time
    or commitment to dedicate to your dream, then you are
    better off working for someone else.

The Entrepreneurial A to Z Appraisal

Owning a business calls for the ability to handle different situations with confidence. The following self-appraisal quiz has no
right or wrong answers. It is designed to help you determine
certain personality traits, attitudes, and qualifications that will
benefit you in your venture. Upon completion, use the appraisal
as a starting point for discussions with friends and family members
about your business profile. Acknowledging your strong and weak
points will help you prepare for your role as an entrepreneur.

Entrepreneurial Quiz

Use the letter *S* for strong or *N* for needs improvement beside the characteristics listed below. Give yourself sufficient time to analyze each trait.

Achievement: I have a strong desire to be successful in my chosen business venture. _____

Belief: I have faith in myself and the service or product I am specializing in to build my business. _____

Creativity: I am able to address situations in imaginative and innovative ways to reach my goals. _____

Discipline: I am self-motivated and can handle necessary tasks, whether or not I enjoy them. _____

Efficient: I am organized and can arrange my priorities or change my work methods as needed for maximum production. _____

Friendly: I am genuinely interested in people and enjoy my interactions with them on a day-to-day basis. _____

Goal Oriented: I have a tendency to set my sights on preset goals and will work hard toward achieving them. _____

Health Conscious: I am aware of my physical abilities and have the insight to work smart in order to preserve my health. _____

Independent: I am able to work alone, if necessary, and am willing to be responsible for my own actions. _____

Judgment: My conclusions about people or situations are generally accurate. _____

Knowledge: I have solid experience in my field and have spent enough time in a professional business setting to know the ropes. _____

Leadership: I am able to direct people effectively while instilling confidence and loyalty. _____

Maturity: I am willing to work toward long-term goals and do not get upset by the inevitable minor setbacks. _____

Networking: I am willing to develop associations with other entrepreneurs for professional support in my venture. _____

Optimism: I am able to see what is right about a situation and to explore its potential to the fullest. _____

Positive Attitude: I am convinced that I can accomplish anything I set my mind to, and rarely entertain negative thoughts. _____

Questioning: I am not afraid to ask questions to get the information I need to expand my knowledge. _____

Resourceful: I am able to find ways to accomplish just about any task I must do. _____

Sales Ability: I am able to present information about myself and/or my business in a convincing yet honest manner. _____

Tolerance: I am able to handle stressful situations with a positive and realistic attitude. _____

Undaunted Spirit: I am unafraid of the unknown. In fact, I enjoy a challenge and accept the consequences of my actions. _____

Venturesome: I am not afraid of hard work to reach my goals and enjoy finding new, positive ways to handle troublesome situations. _____

Well Balanced: I generally maintain a sense of humor when things don't work out as expected. _____

Expressive: I am able to express ideas and feelings clearly and logically, both orally and in written form. _____

Youthful Nature: I am capable of tackling work with enthusiasm and a high level of energy.

_____

Zest: I look forward to enjoying my business, the people I will be dealing with, and the resulting fruits of my labor.

_____

Scoring

Although this is merely a tool to provide you with information about your entrepreneurial profile, there are immediate clues to your future as a business owner in the responses you have given.

Add up your number of *S* responses and read the following interpretation that corresponds to the number you scored.

- ♦ **15+:** There is a good possibility that you have been involved in your own business in the past or, at least, have worked in a managerial capacity for someone else. You have the positive personality traits required to be a successful business owner.

- ♦ **8–14:** You are basically a positive and directed person and should not have any problem with improving certain areas to increase your personal business success potential.

- ♦ **0–7:** This is an indication that finding a complementary business partner who can support your goals may be an option worth considering.

Notes

Key Points

_____

_____

_____

_____

_____

_____

Personal Thoughts

_____

_____

_____

_____

_____

Additional Research

_____

_____

_____

_____

_____

_____

3

STARTING YOUR CHILDCARE BUSINESS

While the childcare industry has been around a long time, it has never been in such great demand. With the changes that have taken place in the American family over the past two decades— more single parents and families where both parents work, for example—there is an ever-increasing need for out-of-home child-care.

The U. S. Census Bureau estimates that there will be well over 3.5 million births per year between now and the year 2000. At that time, there will be almost 17 million children under the age of five years old!

The result will be a continuing increase in the potential for people who are seriously interested in getting into the childcare business. And, for those who want to operate a childcare service out of their homes, the profit potential is particularly good because of the low overhead.

Overview of the Childcare Business

This is a labor intensive business with strong income potential and steady growth. It does not lend itself to absentee ownership and can be started from home with the owner as sole employee.

Minimum Start-up Investment: $500

Average Start-up Investment: $5,000

High Start-up Investment: $20,000-$35,000

Break-even Point: Six months to one year

Average Annual Gross Revenues: $15,000-$75,000

Potential Annual Gross Revenues: $100,000

While the demand for these services is quite high—which means you'll do quite well if you take the right steps—childcare is a service that involves a number of regulatory, bureaucratic, and ethical considerations.

Unlike other businesses, such as mail-order sales, where profit is the primary consideration, a childcare service must be concerned, first and foremost, with the children's welfare...which is what makes childcare a special business for special people. It is not an endeavor for someone strictly interested in making a quick profit.

Childcare programs vary in scope of services provided, but the business generally involves either full-day care (for working parents), drop-in care (for, say, parents' shopping or evenings out), or extended care (for parents who have to leave town for a period of time). You'll probably find yourself providing a combination of these three at one time or another.

Normally, childcare facilities operate during business hours, with extended hours to take parents' travel time and overtime emergencies into account. Typically, hours would run from 7:30 a.m. to 6 p.m.

Deciding on what type of childcare you provide is the easiest part of starting the business. From that point, things can get involved. Some years ago the process was basically as simple as deciding you wanted to start a childcare business and throwing open your doors.

Today the prospective childcare provider must be concerned with such things as licensing and registration, nutrition, safety, sanitation, recordkeeping, and the list goes on...long enough, perhaps, to daunt anyone who isn't absolutely sure a childcare program is the business for them.

Qualifications

While there are certain courses of study available through colleges and universities–child development, for example–that might prepare one for running a childcare program, there are no defined professional criteria that are used to select caregivers. In many cases, successful day-care centers have been started by people who basically love children, have tremendous patience with them and enjoy helping them during the early developmental stages.

One way to find out whether you have what it takes to run the business is to interview yourself for the job. Ask yourself the following questions to see if you would hire *yourself* to run your day-care program:

1. Do you project an attitude of acceptance toward children?
2. Do children, in general, respond favorably to you?
3. Do you apply methods fairly and consistently?
4. Do you maintain reasonable expectations for children?
5. Do you accept the environment children create for the activity?
6. Can you maintain emotional stability?
7. Do you discourage unnecessary dependence?
8. Can you communicate effectively with parents about their kids, e.g., discussing a behavioral problem without the parent feeling defensive?

Being able to answer "yes" to the above questions is probably as important–if not more vital–than any credentials or specific skills you may or may not have. When asking yourself if you can provide good childcare, apply the same criteria used by most states in determining minimum requirements:

- ◆ Is the day-care facility free of health or safety hazards?
- ◆ Are the children protected from physical or emotional harm, so that they have a chance to grow and develop in a healthy way?
- ◆ Does each child have enough room in which to play, eat and nap?
- ◆ Are there adequate restroom facilities?
- ◆ Have staff members been interviewed and their backgrounds investigated to ensure that they can provide the proper care and training?

Profit Potential

As with any business, how much money you make will depend on a number of variables, including the following:

- ◆ the number of children you care for
- ◆ whether or not you have a staff
- ◆ what staff/child ratio is required by your state
- ◆ how you control expenses and start-up costs
- ◆ whether you operate out of your home or rent a commercial location
- ◆ the local demand for your service

While you can certainly make a comfortable living as a childcare provider, you will not become exceedingly rich at it. One of the most important things to remember about starting a day-care center is that it must be looked at in many ways as a labor of love.

We have talked with childcare center owner/operators who are grossing $75,000 to $100,000 per year; however, they are well-established in a highly populated area. Their fully staffed and equipped centers are more like preschools in that they offer some instruction in reading, learning the alphabet and simple arithmetic. The minimum number of children they typically have in attendance is 20, while one had as many as 35 at any given time.

The more usual situation we ran across was the home-based caregiver who handles a maximum of six to eight babies or toddlers by themselves. In this case, we found owners grossing an average of $25,000 per year. Because of limited overhead expenses, they were enjoying net profits of between $18,000 and $20,000!

A realistic expectation for your first year of operation might be gross revenues of about $12,000, which raises an important point: You should not expect to make a great deal of money overnight. It is best to start small and work your way up.

But even when well established, childcare businesses are not generally big money-makers, unless you get to the point where you can set up a commercial location, hire staff and offer comprehensive service. If, as a home-based caregiver, you gross $40,000 a year, you can figure that you're doing exceptionally well.

Children think not of what is past, nor what is to come, but enjoy the present time, which few of us do.

Jean de La Bruyere

To put that first figure— $12,000—in perspective, let's look at a typical scenario for the first-year program: We'll say that you are caring for four children full-time at a fee of $250 per month per child. That gives you $1,000 per month, times 12 months which equals $12,000. This figure is adjusted after taxes and expenses to get your net income.

Managing the Business

One of the first tasks in starting your business is to determine the level of need for childcare services in your area. It is necessary to investigate other day-care homes currently in operation to see what they offer, and how you can match or better their operation.

Another excellent means of gauging day-care needs in your area—as well as to get a general picture of how your community is changing—is to look at U.S. Census data at your local library. The Census is taken every ten years, and provides such information as family size, ages, and other demographic information that can help you determine what services to offer.

Depending on what your research tells you, you may want to limit your childcare to a specific age group or time of day. You may do better just watching infants or toddlers, or perhaps providing care only before and after school. Again, check for such specialization when investigating other day-care homes in your area.

Something you need to keep in mind as you're thinking about your business, and watching those of others, is what responsibilities you have as a childcare provider. There are many. Probably many more responsibilities, and of more consequence, than any other business you could open, because your "stock-in-trade"—a child—is a precious commodity.

While a comprehensive list of your responsibilities to children and parents could itself fill a book, here is a brief compilation of what you are ethically and morally obligated to provide as a childcare operator.

Responsibilities of the Care Giver

◆ Be involved with the children, help them, and supervise them at play and during instructional exercises

◆ Keep the children tidy and reasonably clean

◆ Help the children settle problems

◆ Treat your charges as you would your own children

◆ Provide snacks and meals, as agreed upon with parents

◆ Never use physical punishment

◆ Be loving and affectionate with the children

◆ Recognize that children are all different

◆ Be encouraging and build self-esteem

◆ Maintain open communication with parents

◆ Talk openly and with concern to children

◆ Understand that children need more than just physical care to ensure their emotional and societal development

U.S. Census figures indicate that well over 3.5 million births will take place per year between now and the year 2000–a positive barometer for the future of childcare services in America.

Many of your responsibilities will be based on specific situations, such as caring for a sick child or providing a shoulder to cry on when a parent's leaving brings tears, and they will become apparent as situations occur. If you have a basic frame of reference that is caring and keeps the children's best interest foremost in your mind, you will be able to handle these situations as they come up.

Parental Responsibilites

The parents also have responsibilities which should be discussed in your initial meetings with them and reviewed as necessary.

The parents should be required to

◆ Let you know when their child will *not* attend and why they will not be present, especially in the case of an illness that could affect the other children

◆ Let you know if the child will be picked up by someone other than the primary responsible party and provide you with written instructions to that effect

◆ Make sure you have everything necessary, from clothing to special foods, to meet their child's needs

◆ Let you know where they will be at all times in case of emergency

◆ Advise you in advance before removing their child from your care if at all possible, so that you can make arrangements to fill the space

◆ Give you consent to provide first aid and acquire medical attention for their child while on the facility premises

◆ Pay your fees per mutual agreement

◆ Bring the child and pick him or her up as when they say they will or call you immediately if there is going to be a change in plans

While most of the responsibilities of both parties speak for themselves, it would be best to put them in a contract. Think of all the
items you want covered in a contract, keeping in mind any legal
considerations specific to your area, then have a lawyer review the
contract. It is worth the expense to make sure you have all your
bases covered.

While a contract is an essential tool to formalize and clarify
provider/parent responsibilities, it simply cannot cover every consideration and possibility. There are many things that can happen
in providing childcare—anything from simple misunderstandings
to serious accidents—and the best
way for you to protect yourself is
to spell out as much as you can in
writing and during discussions before taking a child into your care.

*Nothing is really work
unless you would
rather be doing
something else.*

Sir James Barrie

Prepare an enrollment form
that gives you all the information
you need about the parents, their
employment, the child's doctor or
clinic, and so on. Then draft a statement of philosophy and a list
of things you will do with the children during the day.

Make another list about how you deal with certain problems—
discipline, tantrums, etc. and give these all to the parents upon
enrollment. Then, if a problem does come up, you will all have
some common ground to look at the problem and find a solution.

Notes

Key Points

_____

_____

_____

_____

_____

_____

Personal Thoughts

_____

_____

_____

_____

_____

Additional Research

_____

_____

_____

_____

_____

_____

4

OPERATING YOUR BUSINESS

Understanding how to manage your childcare service is as important to your success as your ability to work with children. With regard to administrative or business management requirements, the records you need to be most concerned with are the following:

1. Medical emergency releases
2. Registration forms
3. Health information
4. Service provider agreement
5. Attendance records

Samples of necessary forms follow, but we strongly urge you to consult an attorney after drafting the forms that have legal implications.

MEDICAL EMERGENCY RELEASE

I hereby give permission for _____
(provider name) to call a physician, secure necessary medical care (including the administration of anesthesia if
surgery is advised by a physician), and to otherwise act
in my behalf to protect my child when I cannot be
reached and/or when delay would be dangerous in case
of illness or accident.

_____   _____
Parent/Guardian Signature   Date

HEALTH INFORMATION

Check with a local school or children's clinic for a standard form
which you can modify for your needs. The main points that should
be covered include an overview of illnesses the child has had,
immunization record, and any allergies or medications that the
child must take and that you may be required to administer during
the day.

ATTENDANCE FORM

This is a simple form that requires a vertical column on a piece of
paper's left edge with the children's names, and a horizontal
column along the top of the paper indicating each day of the
month.

Just draw lines down and across the page to create columns,
then put in a check mark each day the child attends. It would be
a good idea to come up with a letter code to indicate absences and
reasons (e.g., "I" for illness, "H" for holiday, and so on).

SAMPLE REGISTRATION FORM

CHILD:_____ BIRTHDATE:_____

MOTHER:_____
           (name)   (address)   (phone)

FATHER: _____
           (name)   (address)   (phone)

If parents are not available, nearest friend or relative to
contact in case of an emergency:

_____
(name)   (address)   (phone)

Child's Doctor:_____
                   (name)   (address)   (phone)

Preferred Hospital:_____

Insurance Carrier: _____

Policy Number:_____

Date child started day care: _____

Date child ended day care: _____

BASIC CONTRACT—PROVIDER AGREEMENT

As your child's day-care provider, I agree to

- ◆ provide a full curriculum of stimulating things to do while in my care, as outlined on the Daily Schedule
- ◆ ensure a safe environment
- ◆ furnish nutritious meals and snacks
- ◆ give you at least one week's notice, except in an emergency, if I must request that you remove your child from my program
- ◆ keep you up to date on your child's activities and growth
- ◆ work with you in planning for your child(ren)'s future education

As parent(s), I (we) agree to

- ◆ let you know when my child will not attend
- ◆ let you know if my child will be picked up by someone other than the parent(s) signing this form below
- ◆ make sure you have supplies and equipment necessary to meet my child's special needs
- ◆ provide work, home, and emergency numbers
- ◆ give you consent to provide first aid and acquire medical attention for my child as needed
- ◆ pay my fees per our mutual agreement: at rate of _____ per _____ beginning _____
- ◆ bring my child and pick him/her up as follows or pay a late fee: Drop Off_____ Pick Up_____

Name of Child:_____ Age: _____

Special Instructions:_____

Parent Signature:_____ Date:_____

Provider's Signature:_____ Date:_____

Getting Ready for Business

Once you've handled all the planning, paperwork, and regulatory matters, the next step is preparing your care site. You probably already know which spaces will be used and how they will be organized, as well as what modifications you need to make to meet local zoning, fire and health department regulations.

The children's safety–physical and emotional–needs to be your primary ongoing concern. You probably know as well as anybody else how many children are injured each year in preventable accidents. Making sure your facility is as accident-proof as possible is the best prevention.

While specific states and cities may have their own safety standards for childcare programs, you can obtain federal guidelines by sending for the following booklet:

Head Start Performance Standards
Dept. of Health and Human Services
Washington, D.C. 20201

Another resource is:

Child Safety Brochure
Metropolitan Life Insurance, Inc.
One Madison Ave.
New York, NY 10010

Keeping the Children Occupied

Once you've laid all the groundwork, you must figure out what activities the children will participate in during the period of time you have them. One of the responsibilities you have is to provide a nurturing, enriching experience for the children, so letting them watch television, for example, is out of the question.

Here again, plan well in advance so you know what you will do once the youngsters start coming through the door. Make up a daily "curriculum" that provides a variety of activities: art, music, play, field trips, and so on. Build the curriculum by observing what other programs do, and refer to the list of resources at the end of this book—many of which are free or available at the library—for more activity ideas.

Set up a master schedule for you and your staff to follow, and plan activities within that time frame. Be sure to give a copy to parents so they have a good idea of the general daily plan. Here's an example:

Sample Master Schedule

7:30 to 8:00 A.M.— Children arrive

8:45 A.M.— Take older children to school

8:00 to 11:30 A.M.— Activities or play, inside or out

11:30 A.M.— Clean-up time

11:45 A.M.— Lunch

1:00 to 3:30 P.M.— Nap for younger children

3:30 P.M.— School children arrive

3:30 to 5:15 P.M.— Activities or play, inside or out

5:15 P.M.— Clean-up time

5:30 to 6:00 P.M.— Children leave with parents

Remember, even if you are doing everything absolutely to-the-letter perfect from the beginning, it may take you a while to find the best way to run the operation and reach the capacity of attendees that you've projected. The secret is to not get discouraged and soon enough, you will be realizing the profits you desire—because of the demand for this service, you simply cannot fail if you stick with it.

The only way to maintain enthusiasm and momentum in your childcare business is to stay on top of what works and what doesn't work and to change routines and plans as necessary. Try adding new activities or services occasionally to let parents know you have an ongoing interest in what you're doing.

A *helpful hint:* If you're doing something wrong, the child or parent, or both, will let you know. While you must make the parents feel assured that you are in control and know what you're doing, it is also advisable to let them know you are open to suggestions.

If you keep your primary objective in focus–to provide healthy, happy, enriching care for the children–you can't help but remain open to hearing ideas as to how you can improve the service. Consider providing parents with a monthly feedback form or holding periodic open house sessions. The more you learn, the more your business grows.

Guidelines for Success

There is only one way to go about starting a childcare business, and that is with a great deal of advance planning and organization, based on the information provided in this guide. Everything you do correctly in the beginning is one less thing to worry about down the road.

Although many childcare centers have been started by teachers who were dissatisfied working for the school system, it isn't necessary for you to be a credentialed teacher to be a success in this business. In fact, in addition to a basic enjoyment and respect for children, the most important quality for success is an understanding of basic business management techniques.

> *Although there are countless alumni of the school of hard knocks, there has not yet been a move to accredit that institution.*
>
> *Sonya Rudikoff*

While it will seem that there are a hundred details to keep in mind as you get started and build your new venture, there are a few very crucial points that you should commit to memory:

1. You are in a business that is generally regulated. Make sure you meet all qualifications and criteria before committing finances. Check all ordinances–fire, safety and zoning–in your area before remodeling or renovating.

2. Don't get discouraged with all the preplanning steps you must take care of to get your childcare business started.

Your reward, based on the incredible demand for these services, is the short road to realizing a profit.

3. Parents expect the absolute best care for their child. Make it an iron-clad policy to deliver quality service.

4. Have a contigency plan to handle any problems that you think may crop up. Don't get caught by surprise.

5. Study materials and books on childcare consistently. Investigate books, magazines and materials offered by the organizations listed in the book's Resource List to stay up to date on such important matters as child development, interesting and educational activities, problems and pressures children experience, etc.

Most people in the childcare business told us they enjoy their involvement for many reasons other than just the money. Taking part in a child's growth can be very rewarding, even though it is often demanding. Watching a youngster learning to handle a unique situation by themself or recognizing their ability to utilize a newly discovered skill is an extremely satisfying aspect of the business.

By capitalizing on a love of children by providing a reliable service to parents, you can't help but reap financial rewards as well in this constantly growing business. Although a childcare business is probably not going to make you a millionaire, it is likely that you will make an extremely comfortable living by providing high-quality care. The important thing to remember is that you must pay attention to the business side, no matter how much you love the imaginative aspect of working with children.

Notes

Key Points

_____

_____

_____

_____

_____

_____

Personal Thoughts

_____

_____

_____

_____

_____

Additional Research

_____

_____

_____

_____

_____

5

EQUIPMENT AND SUPPLIES

Office needs in this business are minimal and paperwork can be taken care of very easily, especially if you start maintaining good records from the beginning. As the business grows, however, your administrative duties will increase. As more children are enrolled, more contracts must be prepared leading to more record-keeping, and a bigger staff leads to more employee information.

When your budget warrants it, start investigating prices on the following equipment and supplies that you will eventually need to handle your administrative responsibilities efficiently.

Desk
Chair
Computer
Typewriter
Calculator
Index card file
Desk-top organizer
Weekly planning calendar
Monthly planning
    calendar

File cabinet
Bookshelves
Invoices
Specific business forms
Stationery
Stamps
Pens & Pencils
Paper clips
Stapler

Buying Supplies

There is almost no reason why you should pay high prices for office and working supplies. While investigating this guide, we checked out office supply discount stores and wholesale catalogs and watched for sales to find that everything needed to outfit your office can be purchased for at least 50 percent under standard retail prices. It should be possible to purchase all of the office necessities listed above for under $300, including a used desk and chair.

For toys and play or learning equipment, we found perfectly acceptable, yet very reasonable items through discount department stores.

Many items you may be able to borrow from friends or family. By watching the classified ads in the newspaper, you will find liquidation sales of hotels or offices which are closing, and can pick up a used desk and chair or perfectly good napping cots, as an example, for next to nothing.

And if you have time and the interest in rummaging through other people's lives, you can find incredible bargains on supplies for work and office at swap meets, garage sales and thrift shops run by charitable organizations. Often, it is well worth the time involved because the savings can be tremendous.

Equipment Needs

Your biggest equipment needs involve materials for the children's activities. Because your business is probably starting on a small scale, you needn't worry about buying the latest, biggest, and best of all possible playthings. That could be incredibly expensive.

Instead, take a look at the following list of suggested equipment. Although it was created with a full-scale childcare program in mind, you will find it gives you some idea of the equipment you'll eventually want to acquire. It also is grouped by activities.

There are numerous printed resources that can give you different ideas for equipment and activities. Perhaps the best of these sources—because most of the material is free—is the U.S. Government Printing Office, which publishes a wealth of information you'll find very useful.

Play Equipment and Toys

Large-Muscle Development
Jungle gym with slide
Tire/other swings
1 big-wheeled tricycle
1 large tricycle
3 small tricycles
2 rocking horses
2 spring horses
Splash pool

Small-Muscle Development
Blocks
Stringing beads
Interlocking wood logs
Interlocking plastic blocks
Letter blocks
Cards puzzles, various ages
Sewing supplies
Plastic hammer and nails
Plastic nuts and bolts

Imagination
Dress-up clothes
Empty food containers
Electric train
People & animal
    play figures
Play farm
Large teepee
Kaleidoscopes
Puppets
Dolls
Cars & trucks
Stuffed animals
Noisemakers

Musical instruments
Toy train set

Creative
Play moulding dough
Finger paint
Crayons
Cutter toys
Scissors
Clay
Paper
Rolling pins
Paste
Felt-tip markers
Stapler
Colored pencils
Hole punch
Pencils & erasers
Watercolors
Records
Story & picture books
Table games

Infant Equipment
Jumping seat
Crib & playpen
Stroller
Car seat(s)
High chair
Floor pads
Play house equipment
Stove
Cradle
Cupboard
Small tables & chairs
Refrigerator

Send a request to:

U.S. Government Printing Office
Superintendent of Documents
Washington, D.C. 20401

Ask for a list of publications in the following series:

◆ Caring for Children

◆ Child Development Day Care

◆ Creating Environments For Children

Again, you may be able to find a great deal of equipment and materials at local thrift stores, swap meets or garage sales for low prices that won't strain your start-up budget. Or ask friends with children to "donate" any old toys, games and equipment they no longer need to your business. Just make sure used equipment is clean, safe, and functional.

"Creative" Acquisition of Equipment

What you pay for equipment depends on such things as the brand name, if it's new or used, where you live, and if you can get a "professional discount." Such things as art supplies are relatively inexpensive, whereas you might pay $300 or more for an outside jungle gym. Check all local and mail-order resources before buying any new equipment. You'll find prices vary widely.

While you will probably need to purchase such things as a swing set, there are some "educational" materials you might be able to get for free.

Check with a lumberyard, for example, to get scraps of wood for painting on or using as building blocks. A garment factory might provide fabric scraps, and a moving company might have some large boxes. Check with a local tire store for your tire swing, and so on.

Think of all your needs, then ask yourself: What resources are in this community that might be willing to donate materials? You'll find many companies are happy to donate used or unneeded materials to a childcare program.

Do You Need a Van?

If you plan to take field trips to the local zoo or other locations, it will be necessary to have a large enough vehicle to transport the children. The same applies if you are offering pick-up and delivery service to parents. Although a station wagon will suffice, a van is more convenient and a safer bet in the long run. It will, of course, look attractive with the name of your childcare center painted on the sides and back!

The market for qualified day-care centers is constantly growing. Currently, 48 percent of all American working women have young children. In addition, more non-working parents realize that young children learn socialization and educational skills by attending day-care centers.

As with equipment requirements, it isn't always necessary to buy a brand new, fully outfitted van, which, depending on the size, could cost from $10,000 to $25,000.

Although, unless you have a mechanic that you know and trust, it is important that you *not* skimp on buying the safest and most reliable vehicle you can find since you will be transporting very important little people.

With careful shopping through classified ads, auto shopper guides and used car dealers, it should be possible to find a sound late-model van for between $3,000 and $6,000. Be sure to have your mechanic check it out thoroughly, however, before making a commitment to buy it.

You may want to consider leasing. Recent estimates we got on a nine-passenger van averaged $350 per month. This is a healthy chunk of change when getting the business going. The decision to lease or buy is one that you will want to discuss with your accountant to review expendable capital and the tax implications of both situations.

Your Computer System

If you buy a computer, the following criteria should be considered: the speed of the overall system and, related to this, the on-board (resident) software that drives the computer and its compatibility with other software packages that you may need down the road.

In addition, you'll want to check the system's upgrade capability (the ease with which you can upgrade components when the manufacturer offers new or revised product lines); and the system's overall compatibility with hardware offered by various competing manufacturers.

Once you've decided on your business applications and software needs, the next step is buying the hardware. Hardware comprises not only the computer (central processing unit or CPU, monitor, mouse, and keyboard), but also peripherals (printers, modems, etc.) and add-ons (such as fax and graphics boards).

In a constantly changing computer market, your best bets include reading the appropriate computer journals, calling manufacturers' customer service departments, and—most important—comparison shopping.

Hardware prices can vary widely from store to store, so it literally pays to shop around. Talk to a variety of salespeople, but don't let them talk you into a purchase. It's your decision, and it's too important to let it be dictated by a commission-hungry pitchman. Take your time, then base your decision first on need, then on price. A low price is no bargain if you walk away with a computer whose memory or other functions are inadequate or—worse yet—incompatible with your software needs.

In selecting hardware, your main considerations center on

1. Current and future business applications
2. Software requirements
3. Necessary peripherals
4. Price

Term Warfare

The first challenge in hunting for hardware is surviving the initial cross fire of computer-speak. If you can master a few simple terms (and can type), you'll most likely master the computerized home environment.

First, a few basics. The core of a computer system is the central processing unit, which among other things interacts with software. Virtually all CPUs contain at least one floppy disk drive, designed for either 5.25" or 3.5" magnetic disks on which text, graphics, and additional data are stored. The main storage area, however, is the system's internal or "fixed" drive, also known as the hard disk, which offers increased storage capacity.

Storage capacity refers to the amount of data that can be saved and is measured in terms of bytes or characters (each alphabetic letter, number, or punctuation mark represents a character). Under one million characters, floppy-disk storage is measured in kilobytes, signified with a capital K: An 800K disk thus can store 800,000 characters. Storage of one-million-plus characters is measured in megabytes, signified with a capital M or MB. A 30MB hard drive thus can store up to thirty million bytes of data.

A low price is no bargain if you walk away with a computer whose memory or other functions are inadequate or incompatible with your software.

In addition to storing data (broken down into files), floppy and hard drives store and load software, allowing immediate access to a variety of programs.

The second element in the computer system is the monitor, or screen, available either in monochrome (black and white) or color. If you will be doing a lot of graphics work, a color monitor is essential. A mouse or other pointer device is necessary for most of the applications you will be using. There is also the keyboard, with a layout similar to that of a typewriter. Placement of function keys and the touch or feel of the keyboard are the major differences between models.

Next, you must consider peripherals—most commonly the printer and modem. Printers come in three forms: dot matrix, ink jet, and laser.

Modems transmit and receive computer data over telephone lines, connecting you electronically with the outside world.

Modems usually are categorized by their transmission (or baud) rate, measured in bits (characters) per second (bps). Baud rates are typically 9600, 14400, or 28800. Modems of 9600 baud and higher are recommended for long documents. The higher the baud rate, the faster the transmission time and thus the lower your phone bill, since transmission time is billed as telephone time. In addition, there is the fax modem, which turns your telephone into a data retrieval/transmission center.

Finding the Right System

The leading-edge computer market is divided into two segments: the Apple Macintosh and IBM compatibles, the latter now dominated by Windows—a graphical user interface similar to that of the Macintosh. Here's where things get both interesting and a little confusing. The growth of desktop publishing has resulted in a flood of products, and it can be difficult to make your equipment choices. The choice does, however, essentially boil down to two general computer environments: the Apple Macintosh or Microsoft Windows for the IBM PC and its clones.

What makes one better or worse than the other? That decision must be left in the hands of consumers. Each camp has its loyal followers. You'll need to decide what system you personally like best. Here is some general comparative information about each system.

	Macintosh	**Windows**
Ease of Use	Better	
Ease of Learning New Software	Better	
Graphics Capabilities	Comparable	Comparable
Price of Hardware	Comparable	Comparable

	Macintosh	Windows
Availability of Hardware	Comparable	Comparable
Availability and Cost of Service		Slightly better
Price of Software	Comparable	Comparable
Availability of Quality Software	Comparable	Comparable
Price of Peripherals		Slightly better
Availability of Peripherals	Comparable	Comparable
Compatability With Other Businesses	Comparable	Comparable

Instead of outlining all of the available hardware (something that would fill the heftiest of computer magazines), we'll concentrate on the variables that you should consider prior to making a purchase decision.

Keep in mind, however, that you don't have to buy new. You can purchase good late-model systems through computer rental stores (leasing with an option to buy), as well as through used computer outlets and private parties.

Computer Shopping Checklist

♦ Will the computer handle the software programs you've selected, as well as the programs you eventually may need?

♦ How much memory do the software programs require, and does the system need to be expanded to handle them?

♦ What will it cost to expand the system, if necessary?

♦ Is the storage capacity of the hard drive adequate?

♦ How much setup space is required for the computer, printer, and other equipment?

- ♦ Is the operating system user-friendly, with easy-to-use commands and a comprehensive instruction manual?

- ♦ What assistance or technical support does the hardware manufacturer provide?

- ♦ Is the monitor an adequate size and resolution for your needs?

- ♦ What does the basic system price include (monitor, additional software, etc.)?

- ♦ What are the terms and length of the warranty, and to what extent is labor included?

- ♦ What kind of supplemental service contract is available? What will it cost on a monthly or annual basis?

- ♦ Does the dealer offer ongoing support?

- ♦ What is the quality of printer output?

- ♦ How fast and loud is the printer?

- ♦ Is the dealer willing to put a quote in writing for comparison shopping?

- ♦ Is financing available through the manufacturer or dealer? At what interest rate?

- ♦ Is a leasing program available? Can you purchase the equipment at the end of the term? At what price?

Printers

Here we offer a quick roundup of the leading laser, dot-matrix, and ink-jet printers. Shop around for the best deal.

Laser. Laser printers work on a principle similar to photocopiers. The image from the document stored in your computer is transferred to a drum by a laser beam. The drum then lays an electrostatic charge on the paper that attracts toner into the areas to be printed. The images are set in a series of minute dots that look like solid lines to the naked eye. Printer resolution is measured in dots per inch (dpi). The higher the resolution the sharper the image. Laser printer resolution is typically 300, 600, 1000, or 1200 dpi. Printers with higher resolution will generally cost more and print more slowly than their lower dpi counterparts.

Laser printers have become increasingly affordable in recent years, turning the home computer into a full-scale type and graphics center.

Dot matrix. These printers produce characters composed of hundreds of dots and are popular choices for the budget-conscious who don't require high-resolution printing capabilities.

Ink jet. These printers produce pages of text or graphics by spraying fine jets of ink on the paper to form characters made up of many dozens of dark black dots.

Base your hardware purchases on current and future applications, needed software, available peripherals, and, of course, price.

Ink-jet output is often confused with that of low-resolution laser printers. For this reason an ink-jet printer is a good compromise between the high resolution and high cost of lasers and the rough resolution and low cost of dot-matrix printers.

Laptops and Notebooks

These lightweight, battery-powered computers can be used as standalone systems or as add-ons to your home computer, in both cases providing system access at remote locations–from the back seat of a limo or from an aircraft at thirty thousand feet.

CD-ROMs

This stands for compact disc read-only memory. It is important to remember that CD-ROMs do not replace hard drives and other storage media because you cannot save your own files to them. (Rewritable CD systems are available, but they are extremely expensive.) Instead, they are used as a means of storing huge amounts of ready-made data, including software applications. They are capable of storing 150,000 pages of text per CD as well as complex graphics and sounds. For this reason they are used to store everything from downloadable fonts to sixty-million-word dictionaries to encyclopedias that allow users to listen and view as well as read. CD-ROMs are standard equipment on a number of systems and are now available at an increasingly reasonable cost.

Going On-Line

Of all the peripherals mentioned earlier, the modem is literally your passport to profitability. A modem connected to your computer with cables and a telephone line allows you to send information to, and receive information from, other computers.

This is called going on-line, and it can open up an incredible world of opportunity by putting you in direct contact with thousands of other computer operators across the nation and throughout the world.

The primary advantage of going on-line is that it turns your computer into an instant research library, giving you immediate access to information services, on-line databases, private individuals, organizations, and electronic libraries. These resources allow you, through the process of electronic mail and downloading, to retrieve incredible amounts of data on every subject, obtain free software, conduct market research with computerized demographic data, communicate with other self-employed businesspeople, and much more.

Additional Accessories

Surge suppressors prevent damage to your equipment when there is a fluctuation in voltage. Basically a long strip or box with several power outlets and an on/off switch, they are well worth the minimal investment of less than $50, especially if you live in an area where power spikes or surges are common. You should note, however, that a surge suppressor will not protect unsaved data in the event of a power failure. For that you need an uninterruptible power supply (UPS). You should also be wary of power strips that are not surge protectors. They often look similar, but their only function is to increase the number of outlets. Some surge suppressors come with guarantees that reimburse you for equipment that is damaged by power surges while you are using the suppressor.

Computer and printer covers protect your equipment from dust, which can sneak into the disk drives and under the keys to create problems. They cost an average of $10 to $20 each.

Screen filters reduce glare from windows or lights that reflect off the computer screen and into your eyes, causing eyestrain and headaches. Although a lower level of light is required for computer input than when working with a typewriter or writing by hand, it's sometimes impossible to prevent glare from a window. For less than $25, you can buy an external mesh or plastic screen filter.

Disk storage boxes come in a variety of styles and sizes. Generally made of plastic, they not only allow you to keep your library of disks in one convenient place, they also help you protect the disks from electromagnetic fields, which can alter and even erase data from disks. Keep your disks in the box and keep the box at least three feet away from electronic equipment (such as telephones, calculators, TVs, and stereos).

Removable storage media. High-end work, especially involving graphics, requires manipulation of large amounts of data. Removable media accommodate the storage and transportation of large files. You will find this equipment indispensable if you must transport files that are too big to fit on floppy disks. There are several types of systems that vary in access speed, compatibility, and price per megabyte.

Shop Carefully

Again, we can't stress enough that it pays to shop carefully. Computer systems can range from below $1,000 to well over $5,000, with many of the lower-priced systems offering all the power and speed you'll need. It's very easy to overspend on technology that you don't really require and that is available at a lower price on less expensive models.

Read the leading hardware and software computer magazines and comparison shop at a variety of stores. Also, as mentioned earlier, there's a good chance you'll be able to find a perfectly good previously owned system at a very reasonable price, particularly in light of recent hardware upgrades inducing users to trade up. Check the classifieds and local computer users groups for good purchase opportunities.

Mail Order

The same principle applies with mail-order computer houses that advertise in computer magazines. It is possible to save hundreds of dollars buying brand-new systems from mail-order outlets, and you can also buy components.

In either case, do some preliminary research before buying. To the extent possible, know what you're getting.

Financing and Leasing

Many of the major computer manufacturers offer their own financing packages, and major computer hardware stores do as well. Of course, monthly payments are required and, in some instances, interest rates may be above those you could obtain through a personal or business loan. Here, too, it pays to comparison shop to be sure you get the best financing available.

Leasing can be an advantage, since it offers the opportunity to trade in one computer on an upgraded model down the line. You may also have the option of buying the hardware at the end of the term for a preset price. Leasing is discussed in more detail at the end of this chapter.

Backup Service and Support

As with any electronic device, computers break down and will need to be repaired. This can be costly, not only for parts and service but also in lost production time. Therefore, be sure any new system you're planning to buy has a good warranty and has a service contract available. (In some cases, used computer stores also offer limited warranties, so be sure to ask when shopping the market.)

New system warranties vary greatly in duration. Any warranty or service contract should cover both parts and labor. One drawback, no matter how good the warranty, is that you'll be required to ship the computer to the service center, perhaps at your own expense. If possible, try to have the dealer sign a statement covering the cost of shipping if the system needs service within the warranty period. Also, ask whether loaners are provided while your system is being repaired.

Service or maintenance contracts may seem like a heavy expense when you've just laid out hundreds and perhaps thousands of dollars on a new system. However, in the event that you need to have major work done–replacing a disk drive, for example–you'll be thankful you made the investment.

General Office Equipment

Desk and chair. If you're going to be spending a lengthy amount of your time sitting in front of your computer, and some of the working day sitting at a desk doing paperwork and making telephone calls, it's extremely important that you invest in the right desk and chair.

Not only will the wrong furniture give you back- and neck-aches, studies have proven that it can cause extreme fatigue and a decrease in overall productivity.

Depending on your height, you will want your computer keyboard desktop to be about twenty-six inches from the ground, and writing surfaces are generally thirty inches high, so you might want to look for an adjustable computer desk that accommodates both tasks comfortably.

Even more important is the chair. It should provide support for the base of the spine, a backrest no higher than your shoulder blades, and a seat that can be raised or lowered easily. A solid seat and rounded cushion to prevent the restriction of blood flow in the legs is recommended. The lumbar support and armrests should also be adjustable, since everyone's body is proportioned differently. The best way to find the chair you need is to visit an office furniture store and try out several until you find one that feels comfortable.

You can save at least 30 percent by ordering the model you like through an office-supply warehouse or by checking the classifieds and finding a firm that is going out of business or redecorating and selling off equipment and supplies.

Filing cabinet. An absolutely essential item is a filing cabinet to keep all of your papers in order. It is not enough to keep a ledger of income and expenses. You must also save all invoices, receipts, canceled checks, etc. If you employ help, you must keep payroll records as well.

Of course much of this information can be input and maintained directly on your computer, but there is still the need for a simple filing system for "hard copy" and those paper odds and ends that must be saved for income tax purposes. All you need is a standard two- or four-drawer filing cabinet to begin with. Be sure, however, that you don't fall into the trap of buying your filing cabinet through a discount department store—typically these are substandard brands and frequently are not properly weighted. We've heard more than one story about drawers falling out or the whole cabinet falling over on some unsuspecting person.

Telephones. In a commercial location, getting a business telephone will be one of the first steps in setting up your business. If starting your business at home, you will likely be using your home telephone. However, plan to install a separate business line as soon as possible to maintain your professional image.

There is nothing more annoying to a client than being unable to get through because the personal line is tied up. The advantage of a business line is that you can hook up an answering machine to intercept calls that come in after your established business hours.

Although it is still possible to rent telephones through certain telephone companies, the best bet is to buy your own. They are inexpensive, come in a variety of styles and colors, and are generally covered by a warranty.

Answering machines. Answering machines are an inexpensive way to ensure that your clients can leave a message when you're away from the office. Although there are still people who feel uncomfortable talking to a machine, anyone with an important message will overcome that discomfort, especially if your outgoing message is friendly. And with the popularity of answering machines increasing, the general public is becoming more used to them and less likely to hang up. In fact some prospective clients may be highly annoyed if you do not have a machine to take their messages when you are out, since it is a waste of their time to keep calling you back in hopes of catching you in the office.

Machines are available in a wide range of prices. Top-of-the-line models may feature voice-activated messaging without time constraints, remote access codes that allow you to call in to your own line for messages when you're away, and a message counter featuring the time and date messages were left.

Copy machine. If you estimate that you'll be making a high volume of copies, it may be in your best interest to invest in a small home/office copier. Otherwise, you'll find yourself spending valuable time running back and forth to the nearest copy shop. However, weigh the benefits of a copy machine against the cost. If it's more cost-effective to go to your local copy shop, by all means do so.

The kinds of copiers available for low-volume use (considered to be no more than 500 copies per month) include thermal copiers, wet copiers, and plain-paper copiers, the latter being the most expensive. Options you'll want to consider include reduction and enlargement capabilities, collating, speed of printing, noise level of the copier, and the cost of supplies such as toner. Although you can find used copiers, you will often be buying someone else's problems. Copiers are notorious for requiring service, so the best bet is to buy or lease a new one from a company offering a solid service contract.

Adding machine. Many computers include a built-in calculator and keypad. The advantage of an adding machine is that it provides a paper record of your figures, while a calculator provides only a temporary display.

Bookcase or shelving system. You will find that your printed matter (brochures, business cards, letterhead, etc.) takes up quite a bit of space. Bookcases or shelving units will keep these items organized.

Office Supplies

Additional supplies and small equipment include, but are not limited to, the following:

♦ Desk lamp

- ♦ Stapler, staples, staple remover
- ♦ Paper clips and rubber bands
- ♦ Calculator
- ♦ Envelopes (manila) and mailing labels
- ♦ Printer ribbons/toner
- ♦ Cellophane tape
- ♦ Ruler
- ♦ Letter opener
- ♦ Office stationery
- ♦ Company stamp, stamp pads, and ink
- ♦ Erasers
- ♦ Utility knife and blades
- ♦ File folders and self-stick labels
- ♦ Wall and/or desk calendar
- ♦ Scissors
- ♦ Pens, pencils, markers
- ♦ Billing forms
- ♦ Computer paper and disks
- ♦ Memo pads
- ♦ Self-stick removable notes
- ♦ Correction fluid
- ♦ Card file
- ♦ Postage stamps and postage scale
- ♦ 3 x 5-inch cards and index tabs

All of these items are available from stationery, office supply, or discount stores. You should be able to buy the supplies you need for under $150.

If buying in large quantities, consider ordering through catalog suppliers. Receipt of the merchandise may take longer, but the savings can be substantial.

Equipment Buying: New or Used?

You can buy new or used office equipment from dealers and independent sellers. Or, as mentioned before, you can find incredible bargains on supplies and equipment at garage sales, swap meets, thrift shops run by charitable organizations, or auctions. Often, the savings can be significant.

Before investing money, do your homework. Talk with other business owners to find out which brand of equipment they use and why they prefer it over other choices on the market. This will help you make the best decision based on your needs and budget.

Also, talk with independent dealers who carry a broad line of similar types of equipment. They can give you insights on maintenance, longevity, service contracts, and prices.

They will also be able to tell you when to expect a drop in price for the item you are interested in, although you can count on seeing sales on major equipment such as computers and other big-ticket items at store openings and during special sales.

Cash or Credit?

Unless you are planning to pay cash for an equipment purchase, you will either make a down payment and set up a payment schedule with the dealer or take out a loan with the bank. Shop around to determine whether or not a dealer is willing to handle the financing at a lower rate than the bank.

Although this method is a less effective way of establishing your credit, it will serve to get the business going. Another advantage is that if you should find yourself in a tight cash-flow situation at any time, a private dealer/lender with whom you have a personal relationship is much more likely to be flexible...without charging you a penalty for a late payment.

Looking for Bargains

There are many ways to save money buying computer equipment and supplies, generally through third-party vendors and mail-order sources. Apple and IBM equipment is sold only through author ized dealers, while IBM clones and third-party peripherals are available everywhere from small stores to mail-order businesses run by electronics whizzes who create their own computers and accessories.

A word of caution here: You need reliable equipment that is backed up by warranty. Whatever your decision on brand, make sure you are protected with a company that stands behind what it sells.

Shopping around is the only way to get the best deal on equipment and software. If you live in a small town, buy a newspaper for the nearest big city and look for computer ads.

Buying Used Equipment

When buying used equipment from a dealer, the chances of it being in working condition are generally pretty good. Dealers have a reputation to uphold and will stand behind their merchandise, especially if they are firmly established in the community. There are, however, several ways you can scout around to ensure that the one you decide to work with is reputable.

◆ Find a store with membership in the local chamber of commerce. Although this is not an iron-clad guarantee, it does indicate the store owner's interest in following business standards established within the community.

◆ If the dealer also sells new equipment, it is highly likely that much of the used equipment has been traded in by people who are upgrading. You may be able to get an excellent deal on an item that has been carefully maintained by the former owner.

◆ If there is a service department on the premises, you can be assured that used equipment has been reconditioned before being put on sale. It also increases your chances of getting fast, inexpensive, and reliable service if needed at a later date.

♦ Used equipment dealers realize that it is not always easy to find a buyer and should be willing to work with you. Shopping around will give you an idea of average prices and will give you the information you need to negotiate. If the dealer won't work with you, keep looking.

♦ Know the terms of the warranty. Even used equipment should be covered for a short time for parts and labor, especially if it has been overhauled or reconditioned.

♦ Ask the dealer if he or she is willing to agree to offer a trade-in allowance on the item you are buying when you decide to upgrade. Of course there will be stipulations based on wear and tear and time; however, the dealer should be willing to consider it.

♦ Contact your local Better Business Bureau to see if any complaints have been made about the dealer.

Buyer Beware

There are other ways to find and buy used equipment, but it falls into the realm of "buyer beware." If you choose to deal with private parties through the classified ads or with auctioneers selling off the inventory of a bankrupt business, you must be willing to take a chance. Although the prices will be easy on your budget, the cost of repairing a malfunctioning machine could result in a long-term drain on your profits.

This is not to say that there aren't good opportunities out there. The secret is to know what you are looking for and to have a good idea of how it should work. Do your research by visiting with reliable used-equipment dealers before you start looking.

Ask a private party how long they have owned the equipment, why it is being sold, and if there are any repair bills that you can look at. Trust your intuition in this kind of situation; if the party seems truly interested in providing you with as much information as possible, chances are the equipment is as claimed.

If you're told it needs a new part, for example, find out what the replacement part costs and ask if that amount could be deducted from the selling price.

When you go to see the equipment, make sure it runs. Test it out, if possible, and measure it to make sure it will fit into the space you have available. Also, see whether you can move it yourself or will have to arrange transportation.

Ask a private party how long they have owned the equipment, why it is being sold, and if there are any repair bills that you can look at.

Before buying the equipment try to find out if there is a servicing outlet nearby or if you must send away for parts, which can be time-consuming and costly, especially when it comes to older models.

Occasionally you will run across an individual who is making payments on a piece of equipment still under warranty. This can be a great deal for you since he or she will probably accept a small amount of cash and let you take over the payments. Be sure to transfer ownership in writing to prevent complications if you need service under the warranty.

Auctions

Auctions are an excellent way to get equipment and supplies at good prices. Watch the business and classified sections of the newspaper for ads about upcoming auctions. The ad will include dates, the reason for the auction (liquidation or bankruptcy), location, time, and a partial list of items. In most cases there will be a preview, enabling potential buyers to view the merchandise before the bidding begins. Take advantage of the preview to inspect and select the equipment you want to bid on. A fee will be required for a bidder registration number, which is held up when you make a bid so the auctioneer's spotters know who has purchased a particular item.

There are two rules to remember at auctions:

1. Cash or a personal check for the full purchase amount must be paid on the day of the auction.
2. Don't move your hands or make significant gestures during bidding or you might find that you have purchased something you didn't want.

Leasing Equipment

Leasing is defined as a long-term agreement between two parties for the use of a specific item. The person who leases is known as the lessee, while the owner of the item is referred to as the lessor.

Despite the fact that you do not own the equipment when you lease, and so cannot take advantage of depreciation on it for tax purposes, there are still many benefits for the beginning business owner.

Leasing lets you try out a piece of equipment for a given period of time to determine if it is the best product for your needs. Although you are locked in to the terms of the lease, most lessors are flexible.

Know What You Need

Of course, the best way to enter into a lease is to be absolutely clear about what you expect the equipment to do for you. The service representative from the leasing company is well-versed in tailoring equipment to the customer, so do not hesitate to ask questions about capabilities.

Most lessors offer good maintenance contracts, as they want to protect their equipment. Check to see what parts and/or labor are covered before signing the lease. The lessor should also be willing to provide technical advice at no charge, may be willing to offer installation and setup of the equipment, and may also provide training, if required.

Payments can be arranged to fit your budgetary needs on a monthly, semiannual, or annual basis. This gives you the freedom to schedule payments for peak cash-flow periods. You can also negotiate the rates and length of the lease to keep monthly operating expenses at a minimum.

Conditional Sales Agreement

Under the provisions of a conditional sales agreement, you become the owner of the leased goods from the agreement date. At the end of the lease period, you are required to purchase the item for a preestablished price. This is often referred to as a balloon payment and should be agreed upon by you and the lessor prior to your signing the lease.

The conditional sales agreement, unlike most other leasing contracts, gives you the tax advantage of claiming depreciation on equipment. Depreciation refers to the decrease in the value of an asset because of wear and tear over a period of time.

You are entitled to deduct depreciation from your income tax based on the value when new, the estimated life of the item, and the value at the end of that estimated life. It is best to work with your accountant on determining depreciation of fixed assets.

There is seldom a down payment, other than the first month's lease amount, required on a leased item, since leasing is generally 100 percent financed for the terms of the agreement. This frees your start-up or working capital for other uses.

True Lease Agreements

You can write off lease payments on your income tax, but only if you have a true lease contract. Under a true lease, the lessor owns the equipment at all times during the contract period. If you decided, at the end of the lease, that you wanted to buy the equipment, you would have to pay whatever purchase price was decided by the lessor.

Financial Lease

The financial lease covers a period that does not extend beyond the estimated life of the equipment. Payments must be made as stipulated on the date due and made consistently to the end of the lease. It usually puts the responsibility and cost of maintenance on the lessee.

Operating Lease

The operating lease generally requires the lessor to handle maintenance of the equipment. It offers the option of canceling the lease, but only if a cancellation clause has been included at the negotiating stage.

The most important aspects of leasing are the terms outlined in the formal lease. Have the lessor draw up a proposal for you, based on everything you have discussed in an initial meeting. If you have any trouble understanding the terms of the proposal, have your accountant review it with you. In fact, it is a definite advantage to have the final lease agreement checked by your attorney or accountant before you sign it.

Your Lease Agreement

Your lease agreement should include

- ♦ The length of the contract in months or years
- ♦ The rate you are to be charged, which is usually a percentage of the total purchase price computed on a monthly rate
- ♦ Your payment schedule
- ♦ A purchase option, if applicable, at the end of the lease
- ♦ A renewal option, if applicable, which allows you to carry the lease over for an additional period of time
- ♦ A cancellation agreement in the event you want or need to cancel the lease
- ♦ Maintenance stipulations (who pays for parts and labor)
- ♦ Substitution options if updated equipment is introduced and you want to take advantage of improvements
- ♦ Any provisions particular to the lease, including tax allowances for depreciation, insurance liability in case of loss or damage, and your responsibilities in reporting a move or other major change

Whether you decide to borrow, buy new equipment, find good used equipment, or lease, be sure to get exactly what you need to keep costs to a minimum. This is especially important during the early stages of your business when cash is bound to be tight. You can always upgrade or add to your equipment inventory as profits increase.

Start-up Costs

(Based on an average investment equipping a home office)

Office furniture*	$650.00
Office supplies	$150.00
Computer	$1,500.00
Printer (laser)	$750.00
Licenses & permits	$150.00
Utility & phone deposits	$150.00
Professional services	$200.00
Insurance (first quarter)	$450.00
Start-up marketing	$1,000.00
Total	**$5,000.00**

*Price reflects sale or discount purchases.

Notes

Key Points

_____

_____

_____

_____

_____

_____

_____

Personal Thoughts

_____

_____

_____

_____

_____

Additional Research

_____

_____

_____

_____

_____

_____

6

START-UP BASICS

Having decided that you are ready and able to accept the challenge of starting your own business, it is necessary to take a look at your overall financial picture. Even if you have a healthy savings account, or feel you can start your business with a minimal capital investment, diagnosing your personal financial situation will help you determine ongoing expenses.

The easiest way to estimate exactly how much money you will need to get your business started and to cover expenses, including personal living expenses for the first six months, is to prepare a *Cash Flow Statement* and a *Projected Expense Statement*. Samples are provided in this chapter.

Preparing the Projected Expense Statement will give you a fairly accurate picture of what it will cost to open the doors and will indicate how much income you must generate to realize a profit. Another advantage of creating these charts early in the game is that two of the required documents will already be prepared when you want to explore funding options; then you will only need to update them.

The first step in examining your financial situation is to ask yourself the following questions:

1. Do I generally pay my bills on time or do I wait until my creditors start sending me collection notices?

2. Have I regularly reconciled my bank statement so I know how much money I have in my checking account at any given time?

3. Is my philosophy "If I've got it, I spend it" or do I carefully plan how I am going to use my income?

4. Have I ever developed a personal budget so I know how much money is coming in, how much is going out, and what I have left over?

These are important aspects of your financial personality that will be helpful to understand when running your business. As your business and subsequent involvement with financial matters grow, it will be vital that you have a handle on your philosophy about money. And there is no time like in the beginning, when your business concept is being formed, to start learning.

The Cash Flow Statement

Use the Cash Flow Statement at the end of this chapter to determine your personal living expenses for the past three to six months to help you gauge what you will need to survive during the early stages of your business.

The easiest way to complete the statement is to use your checkbook register or sales receipts as research tools. If your expenses are relatively consistent from month to month, you should be able to get an overview by analyzing one month. A more accurate picture will emerge if you break down income and expenses for three to six months to account for periodic payments, such as taxes, insurance, and seasonal spending.

Using the samples provided, fill in the amounts in each category from your checkbook register or receipts. Use a separate sheet for every month that you are analyzing. For miscellaneous spending, a standard calculation is 5 percent of monthly income.

Add up each month's expenses, total them all, and then divide that figure by the number of months you are analyzing. This will give you an average monthly expense figure.

Follow the same procedure for income. You can then subtract your expenses from your income to see where you stand. If you have computed your figures accurately, you might run across a few surprises. It isn't unusual to discover that we spend more money than we realize, often on unnecessary purchases. You may be able to see some areas where you can cut back.

The main points, however, are that you now know

1. How much or whether you can afford to invest your own money in your new business

2. What it costs for you to live comfortably, which will help you set income goals for the business

A six-month cost projection will be a good indicator not only of expenses near-term, but the kinds of profits you can expect as the business gets underway.

Start-up Costs

Every business owner has specific standards about how he or she wants to run the operation. One person may feel perfectly comfortable waiting to order business cards until there is a profit. Another wouldn't dream of opening the doors without cards, brochures, and letterhead already printed.

You will have your own ideas about what you need before opening your business. Then you must find out what it will cost and, if at all possible, prepare the Start-up Costs Worksheet at the end of this chapter.

It is also advisable to figure how much it will cost to run the business for three to six months, using the sample Projected Expense Statement. A six-month projection should give you the opportunity to determine your profits down the line.

Preparing the Start-up Costs Worksheet and Projected Expense Statement involves conducting some research. For example, to estimate the cost of business cards or letterhead stationery, contact several printers or copy shops in your area and obtain quotes. Call the local newspaper for prices on different types of ads, including display and classified.

An insurance agent will be able to give you an estimate on liability coverage. Check with the telephone company for information and rates on installing a phone line.

You can also start to shop around to find the best prices on office supplies, equipment, and materials needed to conduct business.

After you have completed your research, incorporate the information on the blank charts. Obviously, some of your figures, such as those for telephone expenses, will be guesstimated. However, the final figure will give you a good idea of start-up and operational costs for the first six months.

Utilizing the same theory, you can develop a *Projected Income Statement* (worksheet not provided), drawing from industry figures available through your trade association or other research sources. This would include all income realized from cash sales, collection on outstanding invoices, credit card sales, and miscellaneous income. By subtracting your total expenses from total income, you will get a clear picture of projected profit or loss.

All of these statements will be requested by loan officers, venture capitalists, and the Small Business Administration if and when you apply for a loan. This kind of paperwork is required to ensure that you have basic business knowledge, a commendable track record, and are serious about your venture. You will also be required to fill out a personal financial statement, available through the lending institution, especially if you are the sole owner or a general partner in the business.

Start-up Costs for Your Childcare Business

The following list will help you focus in on anticipated start-up expenses for your childcare center. In projecting your start-up expenses, you must be thinking not only about what you feel to be important, but also any regulatory guidelines you are bound to follow.

♦ **Advertising:** These costs include such things as classified and display ads, direct mail, sign, etc.

♦ **Printing:** Everything from forms to stationery to flyers.

♦ **Office Equipment:** Your needs will be limited, but you will want a desk, chair, filing cabinet, bookcase, typewriter or computer, adding machine, and so on.

♦ **Office Supplies:** The usual items, like filing folders, stapler, ruler, calendar, tape, markers, bookkeeping forms, etc.

♦ **Maintenance Supplies:** You'll be doing more cleaning and, therefore, will need mops, buckets, cleaning supplies, laundry detergent, etc.

♦ **Professional Fees:** You will want to consult with an accountant, a lawyer, and an insurance agent before starting up. There are also license and registration fees at state and local levels.

Babies do not want to hear about babies; they like to be told of giants and castles, and of something that can stretch and stimulate their little minds.

Samuel Johnson

♦ **Renovation Expenses:** You may need to make additions or changes to your home or commercial location to accommodate a steady presence of children. Costs here include plumbers, carpenters, painters, etc.

♦ **Classroom Expenses:** Costs here are for all the materials you'll use to educate, entertain and otherwise occupy your charges. Everything from tables to a blackboard to a record player fall into this category.

♦ **Miscellaneous:** This includes subscriptions to parenting magazines, first-aid kit, expenses for field trips, interest on borrowed money, sundry supplies...this is the catch-all category.

It is possible to start a home-based childcare operation for a minimum start-up investment of $500, which covers initial licensing fees for your area, a low-budget advertising and promotional campaign and the cost of toys and equipment you need to get started.

Starting Small

Many childcare centers have actually started for even less than $500 by limiting the age of their charges to children under a year old, which means a minimum of developmental toys and outdoor play equipment.

Dianne's Day-Care, located in a booming Northwestern city, started five years ago when Dianne decided she wanted to supplement her husband's income after their baby was born.

She didn't spend a penny on advertising, but simply spread the word that she was looking for "clients" by telling all of her friends who had children or worked in offices to spread the word. She also visited "Mommy and Me" programs at local YMCA's and community centers to let the new mothers in attendance know her service was available. Within two months, she was caring for five infants, in addition to her own, at $450 per month, bringing in a substantial income, and knew she would be able to watch her own baby grow. And, since all of the mothers were willing to provide their own disposable diapers, formulas and toys, she enjoyed a profit margin of almost 90 percent.

As her charges grew, she slowly expanded the business to accommodate their increased capabilities. Five years later, Dianne's Day-Care is a successful business located in a commercial facility with a full-time staff of eight qualified assistants.

If, however, Dianne had started the business at the level to which it has currently evolved, her start-up expenses would have been closer to $25,000. This would cover rent, employee salaries, play and teaching equipment and leasehold improvements including decorating, an efficiency kitchen, nap room and bathroom facilities.

Start-up Costs

(Based on Average Investment: Home-Based Center)

Basic play equipment including a new jungle gym & furnished playhouse	$1,500.00
Kitchen supplies & equipment (lunches/snacks)	400.00
Office supplies & equipment	450.00
Licenses, permits, fictitious name statement	250.00
Toys, books, record, art supplies, etc.	650.00
Storage units for toys & games	150.00
Legal & accounting start-up consultations	200.00
Insurance (3 months)	650.00
Advertising & promotion	750.00
Total	**$5,000.00**

For Higher Investment Start-up in a Commericial Location, add:

Rent (first & last)	$2,000.00
Utility & telephone deposits	250.00
Leasehold improvements	3,000.00
Trained childcare staff (monthly salary for 3)	4,000.00
Van or station wagon (new, includes insurance)	12,000.00
Total	**$26,250.00**

Projected Expense Statement

Months:	1st	2nd	3rd	4th	5th	6th
Rent						
Utilities						
Telephone						
Insurance						
Professional services						
Taxes & licenses						
Advertising						
Office supplies						
Office equipment						
Inventory						
Business auto expense						
Travel expense						
Entertainment						
Dues & subscriptions						
Salaries						
Owner's draw						
Loan payments						
Interest payments						
Miscellaneous						
TOTALS						

Cash Flow Statement
Month of _____

Income		Expenses	
Wages	$_____	Rent or mortgage	$_____
Miscellaneous	$_____	Auto loan	$_____
		Gas & auto repairs	$_____
TOTAL	$_____	Auto insurance	$_____
		Life insurance	$_____
		Medical insurance	$_____
Savings	$_____	Homeowner's insurance	$_____
		Taxes	$_____
Credit Line	$_____	Loan payments	$_____
		Food: At home	$_____
		Food: Dining out	$_____
Home Equity	$_____	Telephone	$_____
		Utilities	$_____
		Household repairs, etc.	$_____
		Medical bills	$_____
		Credit card payments	$_____
		Interest expense	$_____
		Clothing/dry cleaning	$_____
		Travel	$_____
		Miscellaneous	$_____
		Savings	$_____
		TOTAL	$_____

Start-up Costs Worksheet

Furniture: Purchase price $_____

        Down payment required $_____

Fixtures: Purchase price   _____

        Down payment required   _____

Equipment: Purchase price   _____

        Down payment required   _____

Installation and delivery costs   _____

Decorating & leasehold improvements   _____

Deposits: Utilities and rent   _____

Fees: Legal, accounting, consulting, etc.   _____

Licenses & permits   _____

Starting inventory   _____

Supplies   _____

Printing   _____

Initial advertising & promotion   _____

Miscellaneous   _____

Total Start-up Expense $_____

Less Available Start-up Capital $_____

Total Amount Needed $_____

7

POTENTIAL CLIENTS

Childcare is unquestionably one of the most urgent issues of the 90s, and it will grow in importance into the next decade as birth rates stay at around 3.5 million per year, and as our society continues to move away from traditional family systems.

Your client base is virtually everywhere. Friends, neighbors, parents from your kids' schools, parents working at local companies, parents at your church...*any* parents within your area of operation are potential clients for your business.

Zeroing in on the Market

Make a list of everyone you know. Even if the names on your list seem unrealistic as far as potential clients go, keep in mind that they may know someone else who would have a need for your childcare services.

Your list will serve you both in pre-planning your business approach and in ongoing recruitment of parents and their children for times when you have vacancies or are in a position to expand.

Start the list by filling in the names of people categorized in the Potential Clients and Contacts box that follows. This will give you a strong starting point to zero in on the market. Undoubtedly, you will think of others who are not outlined here.

Potential Clients and Contacts

♦ Immediate family members

♦ Friends

♦ Acquaintances from work, school, church or social groups

♦ People from the market, the gas station, the drugstore, and other local retailers you frequent

♦ Your mail carrier, and landlord

♦ Sport or hobby friends and acquaintances

♦ Your doctor, dentist, banker, plumber, gardener, favorite waiter, waitress, or other service providers

♦ Owners and managers of baby furniture stores, infant and children's clothing shops, and toy stores

♦ Members of local clubs and organizations

Talk to everyone on your list to find out whether they have a need for childcare services themselves or if they know of anyone else who might be a potential client. Hand out business cards and flyers and ask friends to pass them along—people love to help and will probably be happy to lend a hand in getting your business off the ground.

My Marketing List of Potential Customers

Friends and Relatives

_____

_____

_____

_____

_____

_____

Acquaintances and Service Providers

_____

_____

_____

_____

_____

Other Business Prospects (local clubs, organizations, etc.)

_____

_____

_____

_____

_____

8

A MARKETING OVERVIEW

Now that you have selected the kind of business you want to own, it is important to explore the need for it. A process known as *marketing research* will provide you with the information you need to develop your business, plan methods of distribution or promotion, and set prices that are tailored to the audience you hope to attract.

In addition, your marketing research will provide you with information that will help when you make decisions about a location, hours of operation, the specific types of services and/or products to sell, and how to gear your advertising.

Identifying Your Market

The process of identifying your audience may seem to be an extremely complex process; however, you can develop a perfectly workable and valuable marketing report by using the following guidelines and adapting them to your particular situation. Basically, there are five factors used to target the market.

Five Factors Used to Target Your Market

1. Population or Demographics
2. Income
3. Competition
4. Product or service market match
5. Desire

---

1. ***Population.*** The number of households in the region you are considering for your business is absolutely crucial, as you must have a sufficient population base to produce the sales you need to generate a profit. If the market for your product or service extends beyond your local region, it is important to identify the demographics for your target customers.

   Equally important is the circulation and age range of readers of the publications where you will be placing your advertising. If, for example, you are planning to sell products for infants, a publication whose readership is largely of retirement age would be inappropriate. It would, however, work in your favor if you were promoting health products or gift items. If you are selling a computer-based service such as desktop publishing, you might consider computer trade publications.

2. ***Income.*** Your potential customers must have the income to purchase goods and services. Consumers in the thirty-five to sixty-five age group generally have considerable income to spend on household items, personal grooming, entertainment, and sporting goods. This is not to discount the over-sixty-five age group, a large and growing segment of the nation's population which, depending on the region, has adequate discretionary income (money after taxes and necessities) to spend, or the eighteen to thirty-five age group, which is a desirable market for clothing, personal, and recreational items.

3. ***Competition.*** Competition shouldn't be a negative factor. Rather, it should spur you on to stretch your creativity by creating something brand new or creating a similar product or service that is superior to those being offered by the competition—through quality, selection, or price.

4. ***Product or service market match.*** Basically, this means that you must be able to attract those consumers whom you have the resources to serve. For example, if your idea of the perfect business involves national distribution of your patented weight-training equipment, you must reach an audience that is receptive and interested in bodybuilding through a carefully designed advertising campaign, and have the financing available to supply and ship the product.

5. ***Desire.*** Your objective is to match your product or service to the needs and desires of a particular group of consumers who will be responsive. It is often difficult to figure out exactly what your target market wants. However, through observation of what the competition is doing, it should be possible to recognize a need.

Market Research Techniques

Large corporations often have in-house marketing staffs who conduct extensive research on a continuing basis to ensure that the products or services being offered are in line with the marketplace. Obviously, this is an expensive and time-consuming process; one that you undoubtedly want to avoid.

Through several easy and inexpensive methods, you can find out everything you want to know about your potential market. But first you need to determine exactly what information you need. It might be population or economic trends, the number of new homes built locally within the last five years, or how many people are active in a particular hobby.

The nearest Census Bureau office and local chambers of commerce are consistently good sources for regional statistics. The reference librarian at the public library can steer you toward other data that will give you the specifics you seek.

The Small Business Administration (SBA) compiles extensive marketing information, in addition to material on operating procedures for specific types of businesses.

Check the *Encyclopedia of Associations* at the library to find the name and address of the advisory board for your industry. Trade boards can provide associates with marketing statistics, management tips, and a wealth of valuable information. Often it only takes a phone call to get more details than you could ever use.

> *The greater the difficulty, the more glory there is in surmounting it. Skillful pilots gain their reputations from storms and tempests.*
>
> *Anonymous*

Another excellent source of information on population, income, and sales figures is the annual survey of buying power published by *Sales and Marketing Management Magazine,* which breaks the information down by county and cities in the United States and should be available through the library.

Media Kits and Personal Contact

The advertising departments of local magazines and newspapers undoubtedly have a "media kit" available for potential advertisers, which they will gladly send you upon request. These packets contain a breakdown of their advertising rates and specifications, a description of why advertising with them is to your benefit and, most important, a profile of their readership. A friendly conversation with one of their salespeople should give you a wealth of data.

The merchants from whom you will be buying supplies, equipment, and products are another excellent source. They can give you a good rundown on trends, as well as an overview of current sales figures for their products. Since they are hoping you will eventually use them as a supplier for your business, they will be more than happy to give you free information.

It is, of course, often possible to gauge what the competition is doing and to glean information from them. There are two approaches when talking to people who are soon to be in direct competition. One is to be up-front and honest about your business plans and appeal to their sense of "industry spirit."

Surprisingly, you will find the direct approach works in the majority of cases as most people are genuinely interested in and supportive of others trying to make it in their field. It is better for everyone if "industry" standards are maintained and competitors have a healthy rapport. And, except in extreme situations such as a very small community, there is generally enough business to go around. It shouldn't be difficult to capture your share of the market, especially if you can develop something unique to attract them.

On the other hand, if competitors are less than receptive, it may be necessary to do some detective work to get the information you want.

Focus Groups

If you really want to go into depth with your marketing study, you might consider gathering together a group of people (family members, a social or church group, or friends) for a focus session to determine if your product or service will match the needs of the prospective audience. This involves presenting your proposed business idea, with product samples if applicable, and creating a questionnaire that calls for specific answers from the group members.

Referral Discounts

Here's a way to boost your income that will make your clients happy to promote the business. Offer clients who provide you with the name of a potential customer (or who have someone call you) a discount on billing. If it results in a sale, give a ten percent discount to the referring party.

This method is often used by companies when they are testing new products and, in fact, there are private companies that do nothing but put focus groups together and set up testing sites in stores, in shopping malls, and on street corners to obtain spontaneous and objective input from potential consumers.

The questions you would want to include on your survey would cover such aspects as how often members of the focus group have used a similar service or product in the past, what they liked about it, what they found to be unsatisfactory, how they feel it could have been improved, whether they would be willing to try another, and vital statistics such as their age, income, and any specifics that relate to your proposed business.

With a childcare business, the questions might include a breakdown of the top three reasons people in your focus group would consider using a service like yours, and what *additional* services they would like to see offered. This kind of information will give you an immediate edge on the competition when you are ready to start advertising.

Analyzing Your Research

The bottom line in conducting your research is that you want to zero in on information that provides insights on the potential for your business idea before you invest time, money, and energy in setting it up.

If, for example, you were considering starting your business in a small community, and your focus group information indicated that only 10 percent of the local residents would consider using your service or product, you would definitely want to reconsider the validity of your concept or figure ways to promote it on a broader scale.

On the other hand, if your marketing research pointed out that 90 percent of the population thought it was a great idea and that 50 percent would have an immediate need for it, the potential for your business would be much greater, and proceeding with the idea would probably guarantee a profitable venture.

Buy an inexpensive notebook to help you keep track of your marketing data. Use a separate page for each category you are researching. The notebook will serve as your personal, ongoing market study to be reviewed and amended as your business grows and the audience you are serving changes.

Plan to update your information as new studies are published (generally an annual event), indicating changes in population, economy, or buying and spending trends. Most newspapers publish synopses of local, state, and federal studies of this nature, so maintain your notebook as appropriate. You should also reserve several pages to record comments and suggestions from customers once your business is established, which will help you personalize the service to the market and keep you a step ahead of the competition.

Spend as much time as needed to feel comfortable about your marketing project. The important point is that the results of your research are comprehensive enough to provide you with concrete information on who your potential customers are and how you can best reach them.

Review

I have completed my entrepreneurial profile to determine my strengths and weaknesses.　　_____

My friends and family have given me additional input based on the profile.　　_____

I am aware of the advantages and disadvantages of going into business for myself.　　_____

Time is not a problem; I can easily devote the time I'll need to build my business.　　_____

The important people in my life are supportive of my decision.　　_____

I have analyzed my cash flow to ensure that I can support myself and my family for at least six months or until the business is solvent.　　_____

I feel confident about my future as a business owner at this point.　　_____

I know what people want as far as my business is concerned.　　_____

I have conducted informal studies to determine my potential customers and understand their needs.　　_____

I have analyzed the competition, know what they offer, and have a general idea about their success ratio.　　_____

I have done my marketing research and know how to get in touch with the audience I want to reach.　　_____

I have contacted the trade association for my industry and have accumulated facts and figures regarding the pros and cons of starting my own business.　　_____

I feel confident that my product or service is a marketable one.　　_____

Notes

Target Audience

_____

_____

_____

_____

_____

_____

Publications to Reach Audience

_____

_____

_____

_____

_____

Additional Research Information

_____

_____

_____

_____

_____

_____

9

LOCATION: COMMERCIAL VERSUS HOME-BASED

Unless you have a substantial amount of start-up capital available to lease a facility and equip it, you have probably been considering starting your childcare business in your home, as many successful owners have done.

Whether you decide to set up the business at home or look for a commercial location, there are certain factors that will work in your favor. Your business will benefit if you establish it in:

- ♦ A high-growth area

- ♦ An area with a large preschool population

- ♦ An area with a growing population of young married professionals

- ♦ A location close to corporate centers, shopping malls, factories, and office buildings

Presenting an Image

You must understand one thing about your potential clients before you try to get their business. You are asking them to trust you with the person they value most in the world. Therefore, over and above the warmth and sincerity of you and your staff, it is extremely important that your facility be bright, attractive, and clean no matter where it is physically located.

Parents will feel much more confident about leaving their children if the floors are clean, if there is plenty of visual stimulation on the walls, toys to play with and other happy children running around. If operating out of your home, it is imperative that you have rooms that are child-proofed and an outdoor area that is free of dangerous equipment or enthusiastic pets that might scare toddlers.

Also, one of the most important concerns about location that will influence parents' decisions to let you care for their children is convenience: Will dropping off and picking up children easily mesh with an otherwise hectic day? Any way you can make the parents' day a little easier will only help your business. For example, you might want to consider a pick-up/drop-off service for an extra charge.

Childcare Tip

It is good business practice to interview the parents prior to accepting their children into your center. This will ensure that you share similar views on child rearing, discipline and education.

Space Requirements

Your space needs will depend on how much activity you want to provide for the children, and how many children you'll be caring for. Think of the activities your charges will be involved with—eating, napping, arts and crafts, music, free play, tossing a ball, etc.—and designate areas of your facility accordingly. Planning is the only way to deal effectively with space needs.

An important consideration: You cannot realistically expect to run a successful day-care program in a two-bedroom apartment or similar dwelling. Children, especially older children who have lots of energy and are developing new muscle skills, need room.

If you try to run your business without the proper amount of space, it will only be a matter of time before it becomes a problem. If you don't have enough space in your home, but you have your mind set on starting a childcare program, think about starting your business in rented property. You may be able to find a church or community center in the area that will lease space to you during weekdays at a low rate.

Developing a Floor Plan

Plan your space needs on paper. Play around with your design until you come up with something that looks like it will work. Bear in mind that kids are great at finding uses for space that grown-ups take for granted, so include open spaces such as the porch, back deck, alcoves, attics, cellars, and so on. Whatever space choices you make, be sure to keep the children's safety and comfort foremost in your mind.

There are some defeats more triumphant than victories.

de Montaigne

For inside play areas, think about the sort of items you'll want to provide for the youngsters. Cubbies, shelving, trunks, storage drawers, wall space, furniture and baby jumpers all affect your space needs, especially if they're fixed items and can't be moved.

Outside play areas, depending on how much room you have, should include such equipment as a swing set, play and eating tables, sandbox, tire swing (if you have a tree available), etc. If you have limited or no backyard space, maybe you can take your charges to a local park for part of the day.

Along with certain space requirements come special features you need to take into consideration. If you have a porch, for example, you'll need a gate of some sort. Likewise any open area; the children must not be allowed to wander off. The bathroom will perhaps need a fountain attachment to the tap, and you'll probably have to provide a step of some sort for sink access. The room you use for naps will have to accommodate a number of cots or beds.

If planning to operate out of your home, look each room over carefully as you design your space needs, and visualize how you must adjust or modify each space to make it welcome and accessible to children of various ages.

A hint for home-based operations: The more equipment you have that can be folded, stored, or otherwise put away, the easier your life will be when all the kids have gone home for the day. If you have a family of your own, you'll need to bear in mind that they probably don't want to come home to the daily ruins of your business. You will most likely do well to include family members in your space planning.

Location: Commercial Versus Home-Based

Childcare could be an ideal enterprise to start from home. However, whether you'll be permitted to operate such a business from your home will depend on local zoning ordinances, perhaps your landlord, or other restrictions. Laws pertaining to the operation of a childcare business vary by county and state. It's illegal to conduct a home-based business in certain counties, while in many others across the country it is acceptable as long as local requirements are met.

The Home Office

By operating all aspects of your childcare business from your home, you can save much-needed capital that would otherwise be spent on a commercial location. That money could go toward your all-important early-stage marketing.

If you live alone, you can basically set up your business anywhere that is comfortable for you. But if you share your living quarters with other people, it may be necessary to use a little creativity in planning an office area in a home-based business situation. A spare room, a basement, attic, or family room can be turned into an office quite easily with the addition of a worktable or desk, shelving for storage, and a telephone.

The main consideration, once you get the business rolling, is that you have a permanent base of operations where you can leave unfinished work without its being disturbed and where you have a place to put supplies and business records for easy access. Do not, under any circumstances, attempt to do bookkeeping and other functions at the kitchen table or on a folding card table. You will find yourself spending countless hours having to put things away or move them somewhere else to accommodate family life.

Setting Up Your Business at Home

There is a lot of appeal in operating your business from home. Thousands of successful businesses have been started in a basement, a spare room, or on the kitchen table. It's true that Henry Ford founded the Ford Motor Company in his garage and Jean Nidetch started Weight Watchers in her living room as a support group for friends who wanted to lose weight. Both of these businesses, and many more like them, became successful multimillion-dollar corporations despite humble beginnings.

Starting a home-based business has provided an opportunity for many people who might otherwise never have the chance to become business owners. Women, especially, have discovered that they can build a profitable, satisfying business at home while still being available for their families.

For others, a home-based business is the ticket out of the world of the urban commuter. In fact, a home-based business is the perfect way to try something new to see how it works while still working another job to pay the bills. Once the business has proven itself and is realizing a profit, you can leave the job to devote all your time to your new venture.

Couples often find that investing time and energy in building a business together at home develops stronger relationships in addition to increasing joint income. For the retired and for those with minor physical disabilities, it is a path to staying involved, exploring self-sufficiency, and guaranteeing that there can be a profitable future.

Start-ups Never Change

As with any new business, whether located at home or in a commercial location, it is important to follow the basic guidelines for start-up, including conducting a market survey, drawing up a business plan, setting goals, reviewing capital needs and projected income, developing an advertising campaign, and establishing a professional image.

Advantages of a Home-Based Business

♦ Ability to start your business immediately

♦ Minimal start-up capital needed

♦ No rent or excessive setup charges for utilities

♦ Comfortable working conditions

♦ Reduced wardrobe expenses

♦ No commuting

♦ Tax benefits

♦ Elimination of office politics

♦ Flexibility and independence

♦ Full utilization and recognition of skills

♦ Low risk for trial and error

A home-based childcare business offers a number of advantages for the business owner who is just starting out. Setting up your business at home automatically eliminates up to 75 percent of the start-up costs and responsibilities required for an office or store-front operation. You are in your home, already making rent or mortgage payments and paying for your own telephone service, insurance, and utilities. (In many instances, a commercial location will require $10,000 just to open the doors with basic leasehold improvements and/or equipment.) In addition, valuable time and energy are saved because you don't have to scout for the location, have utilities installed, and decorate the premises.

Getting Your Feet Wet

A home-based business gives you the opportunity to test the waters with a minimum of risk. This is especially beneficial to first-time entrepreneurs, who may prefer to learn and grow with the business in the comfort of home without the pressures that operating out of a commercial location often bring.

As a hedge against inflation, the home-based business is a natural. In addition to low start-up, tax deductions for use of a home office and business expenses provide relief from a seemingly endless outflow of cash spent on mortgage or rent payments. You must, however, be aware of the tax laws, which allow deductions only for that part of the home "used exclusively and regularly" for business and limited to a modified net income of the business.

After the business is running smoothly, you will find that the potential to earn money is greater because of reduced overhead. Your production will increase because you have more control over your schedule and fewer of the typical interruptions that arise in a commercial setting. Of course, as with any business arrangement, there are also disadvantages to setting up your business in your home. By recognizing them, however, it is possible to address and minimize the problems before they come up.

Getting Down to Work

One of the biggest problems faced by home-based entrepreneurs is being able to establish a productive work schedule. There are different types of interruptions that come up in a home environment, including visits from friends and neighbors, household chores that need to be done, the temptations of television shows or the daily newspaper when there is work to be done, and the fact that there is no one around to spur you on.

A helpful suggestion for getting down to work is to dress in the morning as if you were going out to a regular job. This alone will help you set your priorities for the day.

The best solution, however, is to establish regular working hours at the outset (although you will have to arrange your schedule around the times you have established with your clients). If friends want to visit, politely explain to them that you are operating a business that requires your full concentration and arrange a suitable time to get together according to your schedule.

It is also important, if you have family, that they are supportive and willing to arrange their lives as much as possible around your schedule. This can be dealt with through frequent family discussions about what you are doing and how the business operates.

Disadvantages of a Home-Based Business

♦ Success is based 100 percent on your efforts

♦ Difficult to establish solid work habits

♦ Difficult to determine competitive rates

♦ Limited support system

♦ Isolation

♦ Limited work space

♦ Disruption of personal life

♦ Clients are uncomfortable coming to your home

♦ Zoning restrictions

Another difficult area is learning to separate business and pleasure. A home-based business often makes it very easy to work day and night on projects or paperwork. Again, it is important to allot time for personal activities. The point to remember is that the work will get done much more efficiently if you are relaxed and rested.

It is also a good idea to have the business set up in a separate room or area that can be shut off from your personal living space after working hours. This will more easily enable you to separate work from leisure time.

Home-based business owners often experience feelings of isolation from those in their industry. One way to eliminate this is to join local groups, such as the chamber of commerce and networking groups, and to attend the meetings. Check to see how many members are entrepreneurs, which will give you a built-in support system. By making yourself available to serve on committees, you'll be able to reach into the community and publicize your business for the cost of your involvement.

Reviewing Local Laws

Before getting started, it is important to check that zoning ordinances in your area will allow you to use your home for business purposes. Since zoning ordinances vary from city to city and county to county, it is necessary to contact the planning department of your regional government offices or talk with your attorney to find out what is allowed, based on the type of business, the area to be used within your home, noise control, tax regulations, business signs, and other aspects, as well as if you need a special permit or license to operate.

If you are expecting clients to visit your home for business, it is best to have a separate room set up as an office so that when they do come to discuss your product or service, they won't feel as if they are intruding on a family. If, however, an office is out of the question, make sure you arrange meetings during times when the family is away from home to ensure that there will be no interruptions.

> *God gives every bird its food, but He does not throw it in the nest.*
>
> *J.G. Holland*

Another option is to go to the client's location when you must have meetings or to offer pickup and delivery service, if applicable. Depending on the business, however, and the quality of your work, client discomfort shouldn't be a major problem, according to a number of home-based business owners we have interviewed.

The number of home-based businesses has increased dramatically over the past few years. The bottom line, as far as the customer is concerned, is—and will always be—reliable service and high-quality work provided in a professional atmosphere by a professional person.

The benefits of a home-based business to the beginning entrepreneur can mean the difference between working for someone else or turning a dream into reality. The key elements, as with any business, are motivation, a needed product or service, careful planning, and the desire to succeed. Just knowing that the expenses of establishing a business in a commercial location are alleviated by setting up a home-based enterprise is enough to push you forward to success, one small step after another.

Utilities and Phone

The home-based business has an additional advantage: Your phone line and utilities are already in place. Any additional equipment is easy to obtain from your utility carriers because you already have an established payment history.

Single-line telephone systems are adequate for most small businesses, but when your business outgrows a single-line system, you'll need a multiline system enabling you to accept several calls simultaneously and switch between lines.

Regardless of whether you need a single line or a multiline system, some options are now available when choosing equipment.

Programmable memory allows automatic storage and instant dialing of phone numbers by pressing a button or entering a code.

Automatic redial reconnects the last number dialed, in some cases redialing at specific intervals until the call goes through.

Speed dialing allows you to quickly access frequently dialed numbers by using a one- to four-digit code.

Call waiting is especially useful for businesses with single lines, allowing you to take incoming calls while putting the original caller on hold.

Conference calling is often a related feature of call waiting, allowing you to simultaneously speak with two or more parties at different locations.

Call forwarding routes incoming calls to a preprogrammed phone number at another location.

Cordless phones are especially useful for the home business, allowing you to make or accept calls from any location in the house. Because cordless phones vary in quality, it's strongly recommended that you research the market thoroughly before buying.

Speaker phones allow you to carry on conversations without the constraint of holding a receiver. One of the main benefits is that you can accomplish other tasks while waiting on hold. They're also useful for note taking and similar chores during business conversations.

Voice mail is a combination answering, routing, and messaging system that can help cut front-office payroll costs (if you have a staff) while maximizing efficiency. Customers dialing a voice-mail number are greeted by a recorded message and given a menu of options: direct-dialing employees in other departments, leaving messages for one or more individuals, receiving additional recorded information, and using the voice-mail system with a rotary-dial phone.

The cost of voice mail has been scaled down dramatically in recent years and is now available for small or even one-person businesses, presenting a first-class image while actually saving you money (not only in payroll costs but in avoiding potential lost revenues from unanswered or misdirected calls).

Long-Distance Carriers

Whether you're a one-person, home-based operation or an expanding business in a commercial location, long-distance service is, of course, essential.

The host of carriers competing for your long-distance dollar, their conflicting claims, and a wide range of services can bewilder the small business owner trying to make a choice.

When deciding which carrier to use for your business, consider the following:

◆ Areas of the country and the world that you will most frequently be calling

◆ Monthly amount you anticipate spending on long-distance calls

- ◆ Time of day you'll be making most of your calls

- ◆ Seasonal calling patterns

- ◆ Whether you'll be dealing only with clients statewide (a regional WATS line would be a cost-effective choice)

In addition, read the various carriers' promotional information carefully. Does the carrier you're considering charge start-up or installation fees or a flat monthly fee? If the latter, will you meet the carrier's minimum usage requirements and are the services offered worth the monthly charge?

Other factors to consider include available volume discounts based on usage and dedicated lines giving you exclusive access to a telecommunications network.

800 Numbers

Businesses that market products and services regionally or nationally have found the 800 number to be one of their most effective marketing tools. Customers who might not otherwise pay for a long-distance call now pick up the phone without hesitation—and frequently wind up requesting further information about services or making hefty credit card purchases.

Though 800 numbers can pay for themselves thousands of times over, the installation fees, service charges, and usage fees can be expensive. Consider carefully whether the potential costs outweigh the benefits. An alternative is the localized 800 number, available for small, highly targeted geographic areas. Consult your phone company's service representative for further information.

Guidelines for Commercial Locations

Once volume expands to a certain point, you may need to move to a commercial location. Selecting the right location is vital to the success of your business. The first two factors you must analyze when looking for a commercial location are

1. The community you want to live and/or work in, based on family needs, finances, your preference for a particular

area because of health reasons, or the fact that you have an established reputation in a certain area

2. The locations available within that community

These factors are interrelated. You may want to settle down in an area with a limited number of suitable business locations available. Or you may have run across a number of viable sites in several communities or locations, in which case an investigation of each must be conducted, covering each of the following points:

1. *The type of business you are planning to operate.* Remember that retail, wholesale, and service businesses have slightly different requirements as determined by the type of product or service being offered and the market potential in a specific area.

2. *The demographics of the area.* You should find out the number of consumers who want or need your product or service and are willing and able to pay your price, the median income and employment opportunities, the age ranges of the major population group, and the volume of retail trade and projected expansion data (available from census reports and chamber of commerce business reports accumulated during your market research project).

3. *Competition.* You must determine how many other similar establishments are serving the market and how their businesses are going to decide if there is room for your new venture. The best way to do this is by making a list of businesses from the phone book that you feel will be in direct competition and, if feasible, visiting their locations at different times of day. Observe the activity levels and talk with employees, who should be willing to answer your questions if you approach them in a friendly way. Often, the same kind of research can be accomplished on the telephone.

4. *Traffic patterns.* Is your proposed location close to freeways, major intersections, and/or a central business district? Is there sufficient parking? Is the foot traffic past the location strong and steady enough to guarantee

walk-in trade that will generate sales and profits? The ease with which customers can get to your location is a major consideration in terms of success.

5. *Your image.* Before you go scouting for locations, decide on the image you want to project, such as quality products at good prices, superior service, and convenience.

6. *The product or service.* If, for example, you were planning to sell high-priced, state-of-the-art European electronic equipment, it would be advisable to locate your business in a mall or on the main street of an economically comfortable community to ensure getting the response you need to survive. Generally, there are specific areas within a marketplace that cater to consumers in specific income brackets and/or occupational groups, i.e., executives, blue-collar workers, students, etc. Consider your product/service and the projected number of potential buyers within the community.

7. *The amount of rent required.* Locations having the highest potential of profit through consumer traffic (such as a prime downtown site or shopping mall, a corner shop, or a store with good frontage) are more expensive because competition keeps rents up to the maximum. The trade-off is an increase in sales and a lower advertising budget because of the visibility factor.

Retail Businesses

The guidelines indicated above are applicable for retail businesses. Poor location is one of the chief causes of failure among retail stores, but, on the other hand, the right location can be all it takes for even a mediocre business to thrive and grow.

Service Businesses

When clients are going to be visiting your place of business, the same principles of location selection apply as are indicated for retail. If clients will not be visiting, location selection can be based on rent, the amount of space needed, and the convenience to you.

Wholesale, Manufacturing, or Mail-Order Businesses

Where you locate a wholesale business depends on your market. If dealing primarily with local retailers or customers, your location should be within easy driving distance of your clientele.

However, if most of your business is conducted through the mail or delivery services, you can base your selection on the best rent available and the convenience factor for you and your staff. When choosing a location for your wholesale business, warehousing needs are a vital consideration, as is projected expansion.

Before Signing a Lease

Unless you're planning to purchase the commercial location, rent your location from a family member or accept a temporary agreement in a location that is for sale. But keep in mind that you will be required to sign a lease before moving in. The most desirable agreement for you as a new business owner is a one- to two-year lease with a renewal option and a guaranteed rate for rent increases over a five- to ten-year period.

Rent for a commercial location is established either on a flat rate or a percentage basis. Under the flat rate, rent is generally based on the square footage of the shop and on the location or, in some cases, on potential volume. The percentage base involves a base amount of rent plus a prearranged percentage of monthly sales.

Your lease will also cover a number of other points, such as the liabilities and responsibilities of the landlord and of you, the tenant; i.e., who is to pay for utilities, specific repairs, renovations, tax increases, etc.

The lease may contain stipulations about the size of the exterior sign you can erect, hours of operation, insurance coverage, and assignation of the lease to another party (a sublet).

Before signing a lease to set up your business, make sure that electrical lines are adequate enough to handle high-volume usage, that you have restrooms for employees and/or clients, and that there are convenient parking areas. Also check with the leasing agent to be certain you can make leasehold improvements, e.g., storage shelves, at your discretion as the business warrants it.

It is recommended that you have an attorney review the lease carefully before you sign it to ensure you understand all of the clauses and to serve as a negotiator, if necessary.

Review

If setting up my business at home, I have

Checked with the city and county offices in my area regarding required licenses and permits and zoning regulations for the home office

_____

Set aside a room or an area in my home that will be used exclusively for my business

_____

Installed a separate telephone line and purchased an answering machine, or contracted with an answering service

_____

Set up a separate business bank account

_____

Informed friends and family of my business routine and specific working hours to reduce interruptions and distractions

_____

If setting up in a commercial location, I have

Investigated rental rates for the area I am interested in leasing

_____

Checked traffic flow, parking, and foot traffic around my proposed location

_____

Determined that my business is compatible with others in the area

_____

Talked with my prospective landlord about improvements, maintenance, and rent increases

_____

Had my lawyer check the rental agreement and any local zoning regulations

_____

Secured the necessary operating licenses and permits from the city and/or county

_____

Notes

Key Points

_____

_____

_____

_____

_____

_____

Possible Locations

_____

_____

_____

_____

_____

Size and Floor Plan Considerations

_____

_____

_____

_____

_____

10

PROFESSIONAL BACKUP

From the start-up stage and as your business continues to grow and prosper, you will need the assistance of several professionals, including a lawyer, an accountant, and an insurance agent.

The best way to find a professional is, according to the majority of business owners, through personal recommendations from other entrepreneurs, especially those in similar businesses as yours, and from friends or relatives. The most important factor is that the person doing the recommending understand exactly what you will need from the professional you will be hiring.

For example, your cousin's divorce lawyer is probably not as well suited to helping you draw up a partnership agreement as the attorney a friend used for help with incorporating his business.

Before making a decision, talk to several recommended professionals until you find someone who can best satisfy your needs for the business as outlined below and who has a fee structure you can afford.

Equally important: Your choice should be someone you feel comfortable with, especially during periods when you find yourself having to call several times a week to resolve a problem or complete a specific task.

In many cases, because attorneys and accountants often work on a particular business matter in conjunction with one another, the attorney you select may be able to suggest an accountant who can properly service your business, or vice versa.

If you're planning to hire an attorney or an accountant, you should start interviewing likely candidates eight to nine months prior to the date you plan to start the business. This will give you time to find a suitable match and give the attorney time to take care of all pre-start-up functions, such as assisting in the structure of your business or helping with your business plan.

Professional Services

Legal

An attorney with broad-based expertise in business can help you with such matters as raising capital; the legal and tax ramifications and benefits of various business forms including sole proprietorship, partnership, or corporation; name clearance to ensure that you are not using a name already designated by another company; legal tips on operating in your desired location; and help you file all necessary legal papers and documents needed for financing, establishing your business form, and so on.

He or she will review contracts and lease agreements and can provide support with collection problems. The lawyer you select should also be willing and able to represent you in the event of any claims that are brought against you or lawsuits you initiate.

Fees

Depending on your attorney's expertise, reputation, and the market he or she serves (metropolitan area versus small town, for example), fees will differ dramatically.

In a small community, lawyers often charge a set rate for the job being done, while "city" lawyers typically charge by the hour.

This does not include the extraneous expenses involved, such as the cost of incorporating, which depends on the state you operate in. Neither do these fees include supplemental costs, such as travel and telephone, incurred by the attorney in the handling of your case.

A good way to determine the range of fees in your area is to check with your local chamber of commerce or the state bar association, generally located in the capital city. The bar association may also be able to provide you with information about a particular attorney's reputation and expertise.

When talking with potential attorneys—and when you have found one who is compatible with your needs—always be sure to ask for an outline of expenses and if he or she is willing to notify you when the fees for a particular task will be exceeded.

Accounting

The accountant you select should, early on, be able to work with you on assembling your business plan, including your projected profit and loss statements, for financing.

Down the line, as your business is being established, the accountant will help you set up your books and, once in operation, should handle your tax returns, prepare financial statements, and offer financial advice regarding tax matters, cash flow, investments to maximize the use of profits, and the tax regulations regarding employees when you are ready to hire.

Fees

As with attorneys, there is a professional association in your state capital that certifies and maintains records on the reputation and fee structures of accountants.

The basis for fee structuring does vary slightly, however, with accountants. Some charge by the hour, others by the day, and still others work on a set monthly retainer based on the estimated amount of time they will be required to spend on your work.

Insurance

Before setting out on your search for an insurance agent, it is advisable to have already established your business form and learned exactly what insurance the law in your area requires you to carry (fire, liability, etc.) and, if hiring employees, what kind of program you'll be offering employees, as well as your own needs for medical and life insurance.

The insurance agent you choose should be familiar with the needs of businesses and business owners, not just the standard life and disability policies. Your insurance needs will change as your business grows and expands (i.e., employee health, workers' compensation, etc.). At that point, you may want to consider keyperson coverage to ensure that your company can survive if a major partner or employee dies.

There are also a number of pension programs and stock-option programs available in the event you want to offer employees the incentive to increase their participation in the company in exchange for partial "ownership" down the line.

Fees

The fees for your agent's expertise are paid from your premiums, and there should be no extra charge for advice or administration of your insurance policies and programs.

Professional Services

Legal
_____

_____

_____

_____

_____

_____

Accounting
_____

_____

_____

_____

_____

Insurance
_____

_____

_____

_____

_____

_____

11

TAXES, LICENSES, AND PERMITS

As a business owner, you are responsible for timely filing and payment of federal, state, and local taxes. Whether you have an accountant prepare your returns or you do it yourself, the task will be made much easier if you establish a systematic record-keeping system (as described in Chapter 15) and keep your records accurate and up to date.

This includes maintaining all written documents pertaining to the financial aspect of your business: invoices, bank statements, receipts of any and all business expenses, and deposit slips.

One of the easiest ways to keep control of the "paper dragon" is to set up a 9 x 12-inch manila envelope or a file folder for each of the following categories:

- ♦ **Paid Bills**—both personal and business

- ♦ **Sales Receipts** of every product you've sold or service job you've performed

- ♦ **Inventory** records based on ongoing inventory control and quarterly audits

- ♦ **Copies of Invoices** or billing statements that are paid, with a separate file for those still due you

- ♦ **Receipts** for miscellaneous cash purchases
- ♦ **Auto/Entertainment** receipts from travel and promotional activities

All of these documents must be kept for at least five years to substantiate deductions claimed on your income tax returns in the event of an Internal Revenue Service (IRS) audit. Make up new file folders or envelopes at the beginning of each year and store the old ones in a safe place.

Preparing income tax returns is not only a time-consuming task that can take you away from the important job of running your business, but also somewhat of an art form. Tax law is a constantly changing, complicated fact of life. It is strongly recommended that you have an accountant lined up to prepare your taxes and to keep you informed of any pertinent changes during the year.

Business Deductions

The deductions that you will most likely qualify for as a business owner include operating expenses such as telephone, postage, advertising, bank service charges, travel and expense of conventions, interest, dues to professional organizations, and subscriptions to magazines pertaining to your business, among others.

Operating your business from home allows you to deduct not only a substantial portion of your rent or mortgage payment, but also percentages of your phone and utility expenses.

If you have established your business at home, you will be able to deduct that portion of the house used exclusively for business, as well as a percentage of your costs for telephone service and utilities.

Again, because of the complexity and obscurity of many of the deductions, it is best to have a professional prepare your taxes to ensure you get the full benefits to which you are entitled. Filing requirements will be determined by the type of business, the legal structure (sole proprietorship, partnership, or corporation), income from the business, your location, state and local laws, and whether or not you have employees.

For example, as the sole proprietor of your business you would probably only be required to file personal federal and state returns based on profit or loss, with the appropriate schedules for business expenses, pay scales, self-employment and estimated taxes, and local business license fees and sales taxes.

State Income Tax

Each state has corresponding filing requirements; however, form and schedule numbers vary. Contact your state franchise tax board or your accountant for details.

Local Taxes

Taxes will vary from city to city and county to county; however, you *may* be required to pay city income tax and local sales tax as well as real or personal property taxes. Check with your local government offices for specifics.

Licenses and Permits

To operate your business, you will need permits and licenses based on the requirements in your area and the type of business you are operating. You will probably be required to obtain the following documents regardless of where you live.

Local Business License

Basically, this is simply a fee paid to the city or county where you are located that allows you to operate your business in that area. Some cities will also require you to pay a percentage of your gross sales every year.

Fictitious Name Statement

This is a registration for protection of your business name. Filing the fictitious name statement will also involve a city- or county-wide search to make sure you are not duplicating an existing name. This can be done at your county hall of records.

Seller's Permit or Resale Certificate

This is required only if you are going to be charging sales tax. Services are often exempt.

Health Permit

This is required only if you are preparing or distributing food in any manner, and involves an initial inspection and periodic follow-up inspections by health department officials.

Taxpayer Identification Number

This is available from the IRS in the case of partnerships, Subchapter S corporations, or corporations. Sole proprietors are required to have a taxpayer identification number if they pay wages to one or more employees or file pension or excise tax forms.

Your local governmental offices or your attorney will be able to give you specific licenses and permits required, as well as the corresponding fees for each as they apply to your business.

Legal Structure

As a self-employed business owner, you are required to decide on a legal form of business for tax reporting purposes. There are four basic classifications, as outlined below. If, after reviewing them, you are still unsure of which way to go, it would be advisable to talk with a lawyer about the advantages and disadvantages of each structure for your particular business.

All businesses, regardless of size, are required to maintain detailed records and file the necessary tax returns. In a corporation, regular meetings must be held. The stockholders elect a board of directors, who establish and monitor corporate policy. The board selects corporate officers to conduct the day-to-day operations of the business.

Sole proprietorships are the most convenient and least complicated form of organization for new business owners, especially in the early stages. As your business grows, you will want to explore the options as a way of protecting your personal assets and increasing the potential for expansion capital.

Sole Proprietorship

This is the easiest to establish and is the structure many small business owners choose. A proprietorship is relatively free from government regulation, as the business has no existence apart from the owner. Profits from the operation of the business are treated as personal income for purposes of taxation, and your proprietary interest ends when you die or dissolve the business.

The major drawback of a proprietorship is that you are personally liable for any and all claims against the business and undertake the risks of the business to the extent of all assets, whether they are used in the business or personally owned. As a sole proprietor, you will be required to file self-employment tax returns and ordinarily would have to make estimated tax payments on a quarterly basis.

General Partnership

This is also an easy structure to set up and administer. Since responsibilities and capitalization are usually shared by two or more partners, taxation is based on each partner's share of business income and determined by their individual tax rates. Again, claims against the business can be filed against personal assets, and financial liability is shared equally by all partners.

Limited Partnership

This structure can be established when one or more people are willing to invest cash or tangible property in the business with active participation in the daily operations. However, there must be at least one general partner who carries unlimited financial liability and who usually maintains a full-time managerial position within the company.

The limited partners are only liable for business debts up to the amount of their investment. Although a partnership is not a taxable entity, it must figure its profit or loss and file an annual tax return, which also becomes part of the partners' personal returns.

Corporation

In this structure, stock or shares in the business are sold to investors or stockholders, who then control the company. The advantage is that corporate stockholders are removed from any liability against personal assets. The most anyone can lose in the event of bankruptcy or a liability claim is his or her stock.

The privilege of reduced liability, however, creates paperwork (articles of incorporation and annual reports for the state tax commission and federal regulators), expenses (filing and licensing fees), and double taxation (the corporation is taxed on profits, while stockholders and elected officers are taxed individually on wages and/or dividend income).

Subchapter S Corporations

This structure has proved to be a real boon for small business owners who want the benefit of corporate protection from personal liability without double taxation. In a Subchapter S corporation, a maximum of thirty-five stockholders (who can be family members) report their share of corporate income on individual tax returns.

The corporation itself is generally exempt from federal income tax; however, it may be required to pay a tax on excess net passive investment income, capital gains, or built-in gains. To structure your company as a Subchapter S corporation, all of the shareholders must consent to the choice.

Notes

Key Points

_____

_____

_____

_____

_____

_____

Personal Thoughts

_____

_____

_____

_____

_____

Additional Research

_____

_____

_____

_____

_____

_____

12

NAMING YOUR BUSINESS

As a pet owner, it is unlikely that you would give your German shepherd a name like Fifi. It wouldn't suit the dog's image, nor would it be appropriate. The same principle applies to choosing a name for your business.

The name you select for your business can be a tremendous asset when it defines the kind of image you want to project. You want the name to attract and appeal to potential customers, to be easily remembered over that of the competition's, and be appropriate to the type of business you are starting.

Today's consumers are constantly bombarded with advertising as they go about their daily routines. Getting their attention, and holding it long enough for them to make an association between your business name and what you are offering, is imperative.

A memorable moniker can mean the difference between continued growth or a mediocre response from an audience victimized by information overload. (It is, of course, important to remember that your ultimate success depends on well-designed advertising, careful planning, and quality products and/or service.)

Naming Your Childcare Business

Take some time to think about this, because your company name needs to fulfill several functions beyond identifying you. The name you choose can affect a customer's perceptions of your legitimacy.

It may serve you best to just use your own name, e.g., Mary's Childcare.

Depending on where you live, there may be a number of other childcare businesses with names that are similar to the one you want. Set yourself apart from the flock. Choose a name that is catchy and descriptive, and then come up with a logo that says something about who you are.

Brainstorming

Start by making a list of all the positive aspects of your business that you can think of, and call on friends and relatives to provide as many as they can come up with. Write down all the possibilities, no matter how funny or unusual they seem. A handy tool for business naming is the thesaurus, which will give you a vast number of options for commonplace names. Consider everything that springs forth from your imagination.

When you have created a list of likely candidates, get together with a group of supportive friends and family members and have a brainstorming session to either pick one of the choices you have come up with or to develop something from the ideas listed. Chances are that within a few hours, you will have a name for your business.

Catchy names are fun to design. However, make sure it isn't so offbeat, cute, or trendy as to risk slipping into obscurity as time passes.

The Fictitious Name Statement

You are required to file a fictitious name statement with the county clerk's office where you will be basing the business. While there, you should be able to do a countywide name check on the spot to see if there are any other businesses in the region using the name you have selected. The filing fee depends on where you live, and must be done within thirty days after you officially open your business.

It will also be necessary to publish the fictitious name in a local newspaper; the cost depends on the circulation of the paper. The county clerk's office will advise you about specific requirements in your area.

If you are starting a business that will be operating in a broader market, statewide or nationally, it is important to have your attorney do a name clearance investigation, which can take from three days to three weeks.

Your Visual Image

After you have selected a name that reflects your business image, the next step is translating it into a visual symbol or logo (logotype) to serve as the signature piece for your business. Often this involves creating a visual interpretation of your company name, but in other cases a graphic symbol or trademark is designed to serve as identification.

Some established corporate trademarks are so familiar that you can immediately identify the company even without seeing or hearing its name.

A good example of this includes the logo of the dog with his head cocked to one side. The accompanying copy reads "His Master's Voice," and it's a good bet that you recognize this as the logo for RCA. Another effective logo is the avant-garde apple that identifies Apple computer products.

If you do not have the graphic skills necessary to design a logo with impact, get in touch with your nearest art association (listed in the phone book or available through local art supply shops or galleries) or call a nearby college or university. Ask the head of the art department if your design can be given as a class assignment or if he or she could recommend a student to do the job for a small fee. It will give students practical application, and the design can be used later in their portfolios. You can offer cash or a prize for the best design. The students will undoubtedly meet the challenge with enthusiasm and give you a number of good samples and ideas from which to choose.

Selecting a Typeface

Save sample logos and advertisements that use a typeface you like. Type is an extremely important element of logo design and can also pinpoint the precise image you hope to express. Type not only presents the basic message, it can play a powerful role in the overall appearance of your logo and can actually create atmosphere. A chart of some of the more popular typefaces is included at the end of this chapter.

When deciding on a typeface for your logo, visit print shops or typesetting studios and look at their typeface books. They offer both the usual, functional varieties as well as a selection of unique typefaces that can really dress up your logo and subtly portray a specific personality such as dignified, fun, powerful, classic, or cutting edge.

Historically, in developing business names, simplicity has scored the highest points. The name you choose should be short, to the point, and easy for consumers to pronounce.

Have the logo and your business information (address, phone number, etc.) set in more than the one typeface so that you can see how they will look when printed. Also ask to have them set in both small (10- to 12-point for business cards) and larger (20- to 24-point for letterhead) versions. Once typeset, you will be able to make a final decision about which typeface suits the image you want to project.

Typesetters generally have a minimum fee based on the amount of time they spend on a job, which can vary from $15 per hour in a small city to $50 per hour in a business area, as high as $100 per hour in major metropolitan areas. That's why it's important to shop around.

Word processing specialists or independent desktop publishers can also provide a variety of typefaces and formats at less expense. Since you will only be having a few words typeset, the time and cost required to set them in several different styles should certainly be affordable.

Business Cards and Stationery

The typeface and logo you eventually choose will be used on your letterhead; in your display and telephone advertising; on all promotional materials, including flyers, brochures, and announcements; on your sign; and on statements and invoices.

They will also be used on your business cards, one of the most inexpensive and convenient ways to inform people about your service or product. Once you have had cards printed, be generous. Give one to everyone you meet and always be sure to carry a supply wherever you go.

Most fast-print copy centers are prepared to help you if you decide not to design your own business cards and stationery. They have samples of business forms, letterheads, and cards with various styles to choose from. Make sure that your company name, logo, address, and phone number are included where necessary. If you have a fax and/or toll-free number, be sure those numbers are included. When someone looks at your card or letterhead, it must tell them instantly who you are, what your business is, and how you can be reached.

Sample Typefaces

Helvetica
ABCDEFGHIJ
abcdefghij

Helvetica Black
ABCDEFGHIJ
abcdefghij

Helvetica Condensed
ABCDEFGHIJ
abcdefghij

ITC Eras
ABCDEFGHIJ
abcdefghij

ITC Eras Demi
ABCDEFGHIJ
abcdefghij

ITC Eras Bold
ABCDEFGHIJ
abcdefghij

Korinna
ABCDEFGHIJ
abcdefghij

Korinna Bold
ABCDEFGHIJ
abcdefghij

Rose Round
ABCDEFGHIJ
abcdefghij

Lubalin Graph
ABCDEFGHIJ
abcdefghij

Britannic Light
ABCDEFGHIJ
abcdefghij

Britannic Bold
ABCDEFGHIJ
abcdefghij

Brush Script
ABCDEFGHIJ
abcdefghij

Optima
ABCDEFGHIJ
abcdefghij

Optima Italic
ABCDEFGHIJ
abcdefghij

Optima Bold
ABCDEFGHIJ
abcdefghij

Park Avenue
ABCDEFGHIJ
abcdefghij

Palatino
ABCDEFGHIJ
abcdefghij

Palatino Italic
ABCDEFGHIJ
abcdefghij

Palatino Bold
ABCDEFGHIJ
abcdefghij

Garamond Book
ABCDEFGHIJ
abcdefghij

Garamond Ultra
ABCDEFGHIJ
abcdefghij

Times Roman
ABCDEFGHIJ
abcdefghij

Times Italic
ABCDEFGHIJ
abcdefghij

ITC Fenice Regular
ABCDEFGHIJ
abcdefghij

ITC Fenice Bold
ABCDEFGHIJ
abcdefghij

ITC Fenice Ultra
ABCDEFGHIJ
abcdefghij

Eurostile
ABCDEFGHIJ
abcdefghij

Eurostile Bold
ABCDEFGHIJ
abcdefghij

Eurostile Extended
ABCDEFGHIJ
abcdefghij

Notes

Key Points

_____

_____

_____

_____

_____

_____

Personal Thoughts

_____

_____

_____

_____

_____

Additional Research

_____

_____

_____

_____

_____

_____

13

Developing a Business Plan

Developing your business plan is the most important process you will undertake in your career as an entrepreneur, regardless of the size or type of business you have decided to start.

A well-thought-out business plan will serve as a blueprint while your idea turns into a recognizable entity, and as it grows into a stable and profitable venture. Too often we hear former small business owners say they probably could have made a success of their business if they had only known what to expect from the beginning...and that is where the business plan comes in.

Unfortunately, too many new entrepreneurs are unfamiliar with the importance of planning, or consider themselves an exception and feel they can succeed by winging it or dealing with problems as they arise. Not true!

Every business, whether a large commercial venture or a small home-based enterprise, needs to analyze its potential, examine its strengths and weaknesses, and determine the future of the organization. It works for the major corporations and it will work for you, especially once you become involved in the day-to-day operations of the business. Having a business plan will give you the freedom to follow the steps you have carefully laid out with regard to budgeting, the success ratio of your product or service, the hiring of employees, and other growth decisions.

Advantages of the Business Plan

Once you have made the decision to become a business owner, you must devise a specific statement that clearly outlines *what* you plan to do, *when* you plan to do it, and *how* you will accomplish the short- and long-term goals.

Not only will this keep you on track, it will serve as an indicator to others of your sincerity and knowledge when you go out to find start-up or expansion capital, and it will serve as the foundation of your financing proposal.

The other advantage is that the actual task of putting your business plan together will help you define and clarify every step of your concept and, if done in a conscientious and objective manner, will point out potential trouble spots that can be addressed before they become major problems.

If all the necessary components are covered, it will put your business on the road to profit. It is a sure bet that, down the road, if you find your business is not generating the income you had originally projected, this is because you didn't include one or more of the basic business plan requirements.

Not a Guessing Game

Like any other major project, preparing a business plan involves time and research. It shouldn't be a guessing game. It will be necessary to ask yourself some very specific questions and to answer them thoughtfully and honestly. The business plan is your foundation, so build it carefully to ensure that it works at optimum efficiency for your needs. And make sure it is typed, orderly, and good-looking so that you and others can recognize its importance in the professional scheme of your expanding operation.

An important aspect to remember is that your business plan is not cast in stone. In fact, what makes a business plan so great is that it invites revisions as your business changes and grows. This makes it a companion in your success and, by reviewing it regularly, a partner in your progress.

Licensed childcare facilities grew 72 percent from 133,000 in 1977 to 230,000 in 1985, according to the National Association for the Education of Young Children (NAEYC).

A 15 percent increase in the number of facilities starting up per year through the 1990s is predicted.

The best way to approach your business plan is to take paper and pen and devote a few hours to coming up with some hard answers. Of course, you will want to condense your answers to fit into specific segments within the plan, including (in order of appearance) Concept and Feasibility, Legal Structure, Product or Service, Customer Base, Marketing and Production Goals, Personnel (your résumé and Entrepreneurial Profile and those of any other key personnel), and Financial Statements.

It is advisable to start each segment on a separate page and to create a table of contents to place in the front. Be sure it is well-written and organized, neatly typed, and bound in a report folder to preserve it and give it a professional look, especially when using it as a sales tool to convince lenders.

Key Questions to Ask Yourself

The first question you must ask yourself is: "Why am I interested in this particular business?" Probably the answer will be something to the effect of wanting to be your own boss and making money...independence and income.

This answer is fine as a personal goal, but it isn't going to be good enough if you are planning to approach potential lenders for funding. They will want to see an overview of your business concept, why you are convinced it will be successful, and where it fits in the scheme of similar businesses in your town or city.

The next question you must ask is: "What is my product or service?" This may seem like a ridiculous question since you know what your product or service is, but it goes deeper. Your written response will include details about the service or a description of your product (preferably positive), with a focus on why customers will be inclined to work with you.

Additional questions to consider should include:

♦ Why do I believe there is a need for my product or service?

♦ How do I plan to develop my business over the next five years?

♦ How much will I charge to ensure value to the customer and profit for myself?

♦ Who are my suppliers?

♦ Who are my customers?

♦ What equipment do I need to start the business?

♦ How much inventory and supplies do I need for start-up?

♦ What will it cost?

♦ Who are my competitors and where are they located?

♦ What does the competition offer and how will I offer something different to attract customers?

♦ What changes are occurring in my marketing area that will impact my business in the future?

♦ What are my estimated sales figures for each of the next five years? (A guesstimate can be based on researching similar businesses in the area.)

♦ How will I advertise and promote my business and how will I pay for it?

♦ How and where is my product going to be manufactured?

♦ What is involved in the production—materials, labor, costs?

♦ Where will my service be performed?

♦ What equipment is required for my service and what are the costs for leasing versus purchasing?

♦ What are other overhead expenses (rent, employees, etc.)?

♦ How many people will be involved in the business and what are their qualifications?

♦ If I don't have employees, am I qualified to run the business myself?

By talking with people in similar businesses, suppliers and direct competitors, and your local chamber of commerce, you will gather a great deal of information, both positive and negative, about your potential business. People love to talk about their success and, if you ask in the right way, their failures.

If you operate like an investigative reporter for a few days while doing research for your business plan, it's guaranteed that you will obtain plenty of good, solid information. A Service Corps of Retired Executives (SCORE) representative through the Small Business Administration can also provide assistance or tell you about resources that can help you develop a realistic business plan.

Show me a person with an obsession about succeeding and a solid business plan, and I'll show you a good risk.

Anonymous Loan Officer

Trade associations, listed in reference books available at your local library, can provide you with invaluable details on industry facts and figures, such as the percentage of gross sales that should be spent on advertising, the percentage that is typically paid for rent in your particular business, and how to price your product or service.

The final item to include in this section of your business plan, when and if presenting it for financing, is a personal résumé, designed to emphasize your general business management experience and your expertise within your specific area.

Describe the job duties for every job you have held, including any special aspects that pertain directly to the business.

If you cannot prepare the résumé, it is worth the minor fee to have it done professionally. The results will pay for the cost hundreds of times over.

Financial Statements

Once you have written your overview and description sheets, it's time to get down to numbers. This is the key to your business plan and, unfortunately, the area where many entrepreneurs get bogged down. But without an understanding about the numbers involved, you can never expect to be a good manager and really shouldn't be surprised if you run into money problems within the first year.

Again, utilizing the resources indicated above—chamber of commerce, trade associations—you will need to work up your financial pages to include the following components, which most lenders will want to see projected for one and five years.

Projected operating expenses. This projected number includes materials, advertising, salaries for employees or outside labor, and other expenses directly related to the cost of doing business.

Estimate of gross (before tax) sales revenue. If the business is not yet operating, base your estimate on research figures from trade associations and what the local market dictates. If business is underway, base your estimate on how many items or hours of service you plan to sell and the average price you plan to charge.

How you arrived at the figures for these statements. Generally, you would base your figures on assumptions made about the number of months of operation, estimated number of sales, and the average amount versus the cost of each sale.

Cost of equipment and furnishings. Get estimated quotes, whether you are planning to purchase or lease these items.

Cost of materials. You need to know how much items will cost for production, if applicable, and for maintenance on equipment needed to run the business.

Additional operating expenses. You should research prices for rent, telephone and other utilities, business taxes and license fees, office supplies, and even decorating costs. Include a category called "Other" to provide a cushion for unexpected expenses.

Balance sheet. This shows assets, such as equipment and operating capital you already have, and liabilities or debts and expenses. If the business has not yet started, this would be a personal balance sheet indicating your net worth, listing all possessions of any value plus cash, stock, and other holdings, minus financial responsibilities.

Leasehold improvements. If you are planning to rent a commercial location or redesign a room within your home strictly for business, estimate cleaning and restoration costs in this statement.

By investing the time and energy into this portion of the business plan, you will absorb the numbers into your consciousness and be able to recognize, at a glance, when your costs exceed your profit margin or when you are in a position to start expanding.

If money matters are absolutely beyond your comprehension at this point, it would pay to hire someone to work with you to develop the financial pages of the plan. There are business consultants and accountants who will probably charge you a substantial amount, or you can approach the accounting or business department of the nearest college and see if there is a qualified student available to help you.

No matter who you find to assist you, however, be sure to stay involved in the process...the discipline and hard work will guarantee success.

Notes

Key Points

_____

_____

_____

_____

_____

_____

Personal Thoughts

_____

_____

_____

_____

Additional Research

_____

_____

_____

_____

_____

_____

14

FINANCING YOUR BUSINESS

Starting your business without having sufficient capital is setting yourself up for problems from the beginning. Undercapitalization is cited as one of the major reasons why businesses do not succeed; however, this simply boils down to bad planning.

If you research and record all the goals, marketing data, equipment and supply requirements, and financial needs of your venture before actually opening your doors, you will be able to see at a glance how much you need to get going, and *why you need it.* That way, there will be no surprises and no reason that your business should suffer from lack of capitalization.

It is important to have the financial resources to cover all your preliminary planning and start-up costs, including expenses incurred to research the feasibility of your business and expenses required to set up shop, from equipment and supplies to advertising and utility setup charges. In addition, you need a surplus to carry you over personally until the business becomes productive. The Cash Flow Statement, Start-up Costs Worksheet, and Projected Expense Statement forms provided in Chapter 6 will help you determine these expenses.

If, after developing your business plan (Chapter 13), you find that your personal resources are not enough to open the business, there are other options available.

The four most common methods include

◆ Starting the business on a part-time basis while holding a full-time job to cover expenses

◆ Taking on a limited partner

◆ Going to friends or family members for the money you need

◆ Applying for a loan through a commercial lender or the Small Business Administration (SBA)

There are, of course, pros and cons to each of these options.

Starting Out Part-time

Starting your business on a part-time or "moonlighting" basis is a decision that must be made based on the nature of the business. If you are planning to capitalize on your skills in upholstering, for example, you should have no trouble building up the business at night and on weekends.

It is perfectly feasible to start small, using your garage or a spare room as your production facility and purchasing an answering machine for potential customers to leave a message while you are at your regular job. When you get home, you simply call them back to discuss prices and arrange a time when it is convenient to pick up the piece of furniture to be upholstered.

On the other hand, if you are planning to start a temporary help agency, for example, it would be in your best interest to go into it on a full-time, dedicated basis, as your potential customers are going to want fast results and will call someone else if they are even slightly discouraged, such as getting a recorded message when they call.

Moonlighting will work with some businesses, but before exploring it as an option you must figure out if your limited availability will affect your credibility, if you really have the time and energy to work at a regular job and try to build a business (not to mention family responsibilities), and whether your ultimate goal is to be self-employed or just to earn a few extra dollars to supplement your base income.

Considering a Partner

A limited partner is one who will put up the money you need and step into the background to let you run the business the way you see fit. You must be sure, however, to have your attorney draw up a precise partnership agreement that covers every eventuality. Partnerships are typically entered into with the best intentions and the unwavering belief that the business will be successful.

Since this is not always the case—and even if it were—it is a businesslike move to ensure that such aspects as decision making, distribution of profits and losses, contributions of partners, and handling disputes and changes are outlined and approved by all the partners.

Approaching a Lender

Once you have your business plan and other paperwork prepared, decide which lending association you want to approach. Certainly, if you have a stable record with a checking or savings account at your regular bank or savings and loan, that is the place to try first. Set up an appointment with the bank manager or loan officer to make your request and explain why you feel your business venture is worth the bank's investment.

Be aware, however, that banks are more likely to provide you with a loan payable within five or ten years, as opposed to savings and loans, which are more interested in long-term loans, such as for mortgages. Credit unions operate in a similar manner to banks; however, you generally have to be a member. If you do belong to a credit union it could be your best bet, as it offers lower interest rates and can be more flexible in lending decisions.

If, for some reason, you do not want to run a loan through your bank, consider talking with other local small business owners. Very often, they can steer you to a regional, often independently owned bank or savings and loan that is empathetic to and supportive of new businesses. In that case, proceed as mentioned earlier and arrange a meeting with the manager or loan officer.

Present your case in a friendly yet professional manner. Be realistic and honest about your needs. Do not underbid because you worry that you will not get a loan if you ask for too much. It is always better to start with a higher figure than you actually need so you have a strong negotiating edge.

In addition, most lenders have a pretty good idea about start-up and operating costs of new businesses and are much less likely to give you, and risk losing, a small loan for a business they know calls for more capital. They will be more willing to work with you if you are realistic and knowledgeable about your needs.

> *Money brings some happiness. But, after a certain point, it just brings more money.*
>
> *Neil Simon*

If, after your first try, the answer is no, ask for reasons why you are being turned down so you can restructure your presentation. Turn rejection into a learning tool to redefine and polish your material and to develop new negotiating strategies. There are always other lenders you can approach, and the law of averages dictates that you will get your loan if the idea is solid and it is apparent that you have researched the feasibility of starting a business in your particular area.

Financing Methods

"Friendly Financing"

The third option, raising capital through friends or family members, is probably one of the methods most often used. The advantage of getting a loan from a personal contact is that he or she knows you, undoubtedly trusts your ability to make the business go, and won't require much in the way of substantiating paperwork, such as complex loan applications, financial statements, etc. In addition, you will most likely be able to negotiate a very low interest rate on the loan.

The major disadvantage, according to entrepreneurs who have taken this route, is if the friendly lender decides that he or she wants to provide input on the care and maintenance of your business. This problem, however, can be eliminated by a thorough business discussion prior to accepting the loan. In other words, choose your investor carefully!

The second problem has to do with repayment of the loan. Even though you have a loose agreement in writing with your lender, because of friendship or family ties there may come a point when Uncle Bill needs that $10,000 *tomorrow* to take care of a personal obligation. You can't possibly come up with the money overnight, Uncle Bill gets angry, and that whole side of the family turns against you.

The flip side of the coin is if the business fails and you are unable to pay Uncle Bill the $10,000 he put up. There are any number of unpleasant situations, so you must be sure in the beginning to think about the importance of the relationship you have with the potential lender, how the best and the worst of circumstances would affect your relationship, and whether you then could justify asking for money.

Commercial Lenders

If you are not able to, or if you decide against approaching friends or relatives for financial assistance, the next step is a bank, a savings and loan, or a credit union. Before approaching any of these commercial lenders, you must have carefully developed your business plan, which will include the following documents.

1. A résumé or statement outlining your employment background and capability to operate the business, plus a similar statement about any key employees or partners in the business

2. A statement of business and personal goals

3. A description of the business, including market research for your product or service

4. Details on how the business is going to be structured (sole proprietorship, partnership, corporation)

5. A projection of profit and loss for a minimum of one year (five years is preferable), which means you will have investigated how similar businesses are doing

6. An outline of how much money you need—and why—to keep the business solvent and to support yourself and your family for at least a year

In addition, you will be required to provide a personal balance sheet that lists your assets (real estate, car, valuable personal property) and liabilities (mortgage payments, credit card debts) along with a credit application that outlines your personal financial history, so a determination can be made on your ability to pay back the loan. The lender will follow through by requesting a credit report from an independent agency to help with the decision.

The main point to remember when applying for a loan with a commercial institution is that lenders aren't as concerned about the amount loaned as they are about how and when they are going to get the money back!

Paying Back the Loan

When you apply for financing, the burden of proof as it relates to repayment rests with you. No one would knowingly grant a loan to an individual or a business that he or she had doubts about. As a borrower, your responsibility is to show that you will be able to pay back the loan according to the terms agreed to by you and the lender. If you have a good credit history, a credit report will indicate as much.

The Small Business Administration

The Small Business Administration (SBA) often goes where no other lender will tread and, as such, is a lender of last resort. The SBA is a government agency that is well known for providing financing to entrepreneurs who have been repeatedly turned down by commercial lenders, which, in fact, you generally must be before the SBA will consider backing you.

After your loan request with a commercial institution has been denied, you can file an application with the nearest branch of the SBA. It is a good idea to make an appointment with a Service

Corps of Retired Executives (SCORE) representative (a man or woman who volunteers his or her time to the SBA-SCORE program to advise new and established business owners). Your SCORE representative will lead you through the complex paperwork required by the SBA before it makes a decision.

In addition, SCORE volunteers are usually straightforward, knowledgeable men and women who will walk through your business plans with you and offer constructive suggestions. Once the paperwork is completed, a commercial lender will make the loan under the SBA Lender Certification Program, knowing that the government is willing to insure it.

We recommend this option only after you have been turned down by three or more banks, because of the time factor involved in gaining approval and also because of the extensive follow-up reports required by the SBA. It is, however, a viable option and one that has helped thousands of dedicated entrepreneurs realize their goals.

Venture Capitalists

Money is available to businesses that are already established and seeking working or expansion capital from groups of investors known as venture capitalists. These groups can vary from a few local businesspeople with money to invest to major investment companies connected with large corporations or financial organizations.

Venture capital is not like a straightforward business loan. It is usually dependent on a minimum $100,000 investment and, therefore, is not exactly suited to every business situation. Typically, venture capitalists are interested in companies that have a track record, a proven position in the market, and a solid growth projection.

And, like a bank or other lending association, venture capitalists want to see a written business plan and a prospectus of future projections. They are looking at your background, the market, the kind of funding you want, and your past financial record.

Since venture capitalists are looking to earn from 10 to 15 percent on their investment over a relatively short period, they will want to spend a great deal of time talking with you and your associates, customers, and suppliers.

Before considering venture capital, we advise discussing it carefully with an attorney who can help you investigate different groups to figure out the best investment structure, and who can work with the group's attorney on drawing up an agreement that protects you. Many venture capitalists will want to own part of your company.

This is an option to be considered only when your company is well established and undergoing rapid growth pains and should be approached with great understanding of the situation.

Other Financing Options

Loan Companies

Loan companies are good sources of funding. However, interest rates are high, and they will generally want to have substantial collateral, such as the equity in your house, on record before making a loan.

Insurance Companies

Your insurance carrier may be willing to make an investment in your small business, using your insurance policy as collateral, or you may even have enough cash value in your policy, depending on the face amount, to provide substantial start-up capital. If this is the case, you will only be required to pay quarterly or semiannual interest payments on the cash value you have taken out.

Factoring

In this scenario, a factoring company "buys" your accounts receivable and advances you a percentage of the full amount due. This is a viable option for well-established service companies that work on a billing basis.

Cosigner

If you have a relative or friend who is already an established business owner or, at least, a homeowner with a solid credit rating, it might be worth your while to ask if he or she would cosign on a loan application with you. Although you are still responsible for repayment of the loan, the bank is assured that, in the event you default for any reason, the cosigner will guarantee the obligation. It is sometimes difficult to find someone who will do this, but again it doesn't hurt to ask, especially if it is a last resort.

Starting Small

Even if you know your particular business is valid and that you have the ability to make it succeed, be certain that your business plan is realistic. If you have chosen to start a business on a grand scale but have minimal capital and little business experience, it may be best to begin a smaller, less elaborate operation at first.

You'll require less "seed money" and will be in a low-risk position while learning the operations of a business and seeing if you can handle all the variables of business ownership while making it grow.

> *The journey of a thousand miles begins with a single step.*
> Chinese Proverb

Smaller businesses have proven to be a great way to learn successful methods, as well as a vehicle for ironing out the many small, often overlooked, details. The profits you gain from a smaller venture can be used to expand or invest in bigger business ideas. And an added bonus is that when you are ready to approach investors or lending institutions, you will be able to show them that you already have a solid track record and a working knowledge of business procedures.

What to Do When Asking for Money

1. *Be sure to ask.* This may seem like a gross statement of the obvious, but you would be amazed at the number of small business owners we've heard about who never ask because they are afraid of being turned down.

   Unless you are independently wealthy and pursuing your business as a humanitarian effort, it is unlikely that you are in a position to run your business and earn enough money to support you, your family, and the operation—especially during the first year. Remember the old adage: It *takes* money to *make* money.

If you run a low-budget business, you will probably get a low-budget response. If you are determined to make it work, be sure you have sufficient capital to make it work the right way.

Fear is often a factor: "I don't want to ask, in case I'm told no." Well, that's the worst thing that can happen. But if you persevere and are serious about your venture, someone will inevitably say yes!

And don't overlook friends and family; they can be your most ardent supporters if you have given them reason in the past to believe you are responsible and determined to succeed.

2. ***Know how much you need.*** Lenders are familiar with the financial demands of business operation and will respect your request if you have obviously done your homework and can talk intelligently about your needs.

3. ***Be direct and confident.*** If you believe in your business and in your ability to make it work, others will be convinced as well. Never apologize for mistakes you feel you have made in the past.

   Simply present the facts honestly, even if it includes revealing an error in judgment you have made somewhere along the line, and assure the lender that he or she will be making a smart decision by investing in you.

4. ***Think positively.*** If you need $50,000, ask for $50,000. Never underestimate the potential to provide. Remember: It is easier to negotiate and deal with one lender for a single amount than it is to keep paperwork and relationships strong with several, all of whom have contributed to the pot.

5. ***Ask again.*** If they trusted you once and you have lived up to the stipulations of the contract, ask again—that goes for commercial lending institutions as well as friends and

relatives. When it comes to borrowing money, a proven record is what it's all about, and if you have established yours, keep it active. It will be your passport to profit when the chips are down.

6. ***Know when to borrow.*** If you have worked out your business plan and know you can survive while getting the business off the ground, start exploring your financing options ahead of time. Don't wait until the last minute when you will be forced to act and will have to take a less-than-favorable opportunity. The same theory applies if your business is already established. By examining your financial position on a regular basis, you will be able to project how much you will need at a given point for expansion purposes. Always be aware.

7. ***Don't borrow if it is not necessary.*** Many businesses can be started for under $1,000. This is called "starting on a shoestring" and can be done with a variety of businesses. Services, for example, often rely strictly on the owner's knowledge and expertise and can be set up quickly and inexpensively.

   If this is the case with the business you have in mind, then try to avoid borrowing money, which can be an expensive and timely proposition.

Establishing Credit

Is it possible to get a loan even if you have never established credit? Yes, it is. If you prefer to pay cash rather than incur high interest charges on loans or credit cards, you can still qualify for a loan based on personal assets or by having a friend or relative with a good credit rating cosign for you on the loan. This puts the obligation on the cosigner, so be sure the terms of the loan are clearly spelled out in a written agreement to the satisfaction of everyone involved.

But, if your personal assets are minimal and you cannot find a cosigner, your best bet is to put off starting the business for four to six months while you establish credit. The best place to start is with a major department store. A store will issue you a credit card based on a very simple examination of your income and employment history. When you receive the card, charge about $100 worth of merchandise and pay it off according to the schedule provided. Within a few months, you will have proven yourself to be credit worthy, which will greatly improve your chances of getting a loan from a lending institution.

Another way to establish credit—and credibility—is to open a checking account at the bank you have decided to approach for a loan. Banks generally require a minimum deposit of between $50 and $100. Make it a point to meet the branch manager and/or the loan officer and establish an ongoing relationship with them by stopping by to say hello when you are in the bank.

Within a few months, apply for a small personal loan, working with your new acquaintance, of course. Make your payments according to the prearranged schedule. Then when you are ready to request a more substantial amount of money to cover your start-up expenses, you will be recognized as a customer with a loan history at that institution.

Notes

Key Points

_____

_____

_____

_____

_____

_____

Personal Thoughts

_____

_____

_____

_____

_____

_____

Additional Research

_____

_____

_____

_____

_____

_____

15

RECORD KEEPING: YOUR BUSINESS LIFELINE

The motivating factor in any business is profit, which can be explained as the money left over after all the bills—everything from supplies to rent to salaries to taxes—are paid.

Building a profitable business is not something that can be left to chance; it must be planned, and a systematic method of record keeping must be developed to help you monitor income and expenses.

You should expect that during the early days of your business, your profits are going to be minimal as you become established. But it is possible, with even simple record-keeping procedures, to prepare yourself for lean periods and control day-to-day expenses to ensure that you are, at least, breaking even. In addition, financial records are required for tax purposes, and dealing with them systematically can help you avoid an incredibly overwhelming task at tax time.

Record Keeping Can Be Simple

Some people cringe at the thought of record keeping or feel it is a waste of valuable time. Usually, these attitudes are based on a lack of knowledge and the feeling that it is a difficult job. There is, however, no other way to analyze your cash flow and make sure you are pricing products or services high enough to realize a profit.

In truth, record keeping is not a complicated process. If you have ever balanced a checkbook or planned a household budget, you have performed several of the same steps that are necessary for implementing a bookkeeping system for your business. And the good news is that keeping business records does not have to be either complicated or time consuming.

We know of entrepreneurs who opt for total simplicity by using the "shoebox" method—every sales record, receipt for expenses, and bank statement gets tossed into a box. This system has two distinct drawbacks. One may not become apparent until tax time, when you attempt to wade through and organize each sheet of paper to prepare your tax return. The other, more critical drawback is that it is virtually impossible to maintain an accurate picture of your financial situation when you stockpile, rather than record, business transactions.

In order to understand your cash flow, it is important to be able to see monies earned, monies paid out, current balances, and outstanding debts.

In fact, you should be able to answer the following questions with just a quick review of your records.

◆ What was my income last year (week, month)?

◆ What were my expenses?

◆ How do income and expenses compare with last year (week, month)?

◆ What was my profit (loss) last year (week, month)?

◆ Where can I cut back on expenses?

◆ Who and how much do I currently owe on outstanding debts?

◆ Who owes me money and how much?

- ◆ What are my assets, liabilities, and net worth?
- ◆ Is my inventory in line with demand?
- ◆ How much cash do I have available? How much credit?
- ◆ Am I able to pay myself this month (week)?
- ◆ Are my figures in line with projected financial goals?

The records you need to be able to answer most of these questions are your cash journal, a balance sheet, and a bank reconciliation. A simple single-entry system, as indicated on the following pages, where you can record disbursements (cash paid out) and receipts (cash taken in) will form the base of your record-keeping system.

Double-Entry Bookkeeping

You may want to consider a double-entry system, which involves recording each transaction twice; once as a debit (simply the left column of the ledger) and once as a credit (the right column of the ledger). For example, if you were to sell a product for $100, the transactions recorded in a double-entry system would be as follows: The $100 would be written as a *credit* in your sales account, since merchandise is going out of the

> *If you can organize your kitchen, you can organize your life.*
> Dr. Louis Parrish

business, and $100 would be recorded as a *debit* in your cash account since money was coming into the business.

This is a complex and time-consuming process that is often best left to an accountant, as he or she will need the information to create a monthly trial balance and other financial statements, including your year-end tax reports.

Single-Entry Bookkeeping

You can, however, set up a simple single-entry system, which will tie in directly with your accountant's requirements, or check out the standardized bookkeeping systems available at office supply or stationery stores, which provide all the necessary forms and documents in a bound book.

Bookkeeping Debits and Credits

Debits

♦ Cash receipts

♦ Purchases

♦ Expenses, such as rent and wages

Credits

♦ Cash payments

♦ Sales of services or merchandise

♦ Earnings, including interest

A system should contain forms for recording monthly income and expenses, summary sheets from which you can create a balance sheet, and listings of legal deductions for income tax reporting. In addition, the trade association for your field should be able to provide you with systems developed exclusively for use in the industry, which you can use or adapt according to the specific circumstances of your business.

The final method is to purchase a cash journal book and set up your own monthly system. (We've used Office Assistance, a small secretarial service that has been in operation for one month, as an example.) Any of the above-mentioned methods are acceptable, as long as you understand the entry process and can read the results.

Make Record Keeping a Daily Task

Short of paying someone else, the easiest way to be sure your records are kept up to date is to incorporate the task into your daily or weekly routine. Many small business owners make it a habit to enter their sales, expenses, and other financial information at the end of each working day. It keeps them continually aware of their financial situation and ensures that there will never be any cash-flow surprises.

The process shouldn't take more than fifteen minutes for normal transactions, and it will save hours of pencil pushing and frustration down the line. What's important is that you'll always know where you stand financially.

Setting Up the Books

Now, using the fictitious Office Assistance as an example, we will examine the various elements required for basic record-keeping duties.

Office Assistance has been in business for one month. Two months ago, Bill Miller, president of Office Assistance, opened a new business bank account with $10,000, his start-up capital from a personal savings account.

At the same time, he rented a small office in a downtown building for $350 a month, but had to pay the first month's rent, and a deposit of the last month's rent, for a total outlay of $700.

His fictitious name statement, which he got approved through the local county clerk's office, cost $10, and publishing it in a regional newspaper cost $45.

The initial month's lease and a deposit on a computer cost him $275, with an additional $50 for a maintenance agreement. However, he will own the $2,000 computer when his payment schedule is completed.

He found a brand-new calculator at a garage sale for $25 and is going to use a desk, table, lamp, and chairs brought from home (value $350) to decorate the office. Phone-line installation was $150, and he purchased a two-line telephone for $79.50.

An artist friend designed his logo and letterhead on a computer for only $25 and a $6.95 lunch. He had his stationery ($35), business cards ($60), and brochures ($23.50) produced through a local copy shop for a total of $118.50.

A 2 x 2-inch display ad in the local newspaper will cost him $370 for a week, and he is planning to mail 100 of his brochures to local businesses selected from the phone book. Stamps will cost $32 for the mailing. Office supplies, including typing paper, staples, paper clips, etc., set him back $45. A journal for record keeping cost $7.95 and a packet of invoices $5.95, for a grand total of $58.90.

Since he doesn't know how to type, Bill hired his niece to work 20 hours a week for $10 per hour on an independent contractor basis so he doesn't have to pay social security or unemployment taxes.

During the first month, he has billed and been paid $700. However, he has two clients who still owe him a total of $400. Bill dutifully records information in his cash journal at the end of each working day. He uses source documents, including his checkbook register, receipts from cash purchases, and billing invoices as the basis for his entries. The following cash journal illustrations are for May (prior to opening the doors of his business) and June (his first actual month in business).

Bill's expenses for May and June were $3,108.75. Of course, part of that is for start-up expenses, such as deposits on his rent and computer, installation costs, and one-time fictitious name filing and publishing. His income for the first month was $700.

By deducting his expenses from his income, he can see that, at the moment, his business is showing a loss of $2,408.75.

Office Assistance
Cash Journal for May

Date	Check or Invoice #	Detail	(Debit) Expense	(Credit) Income
5/1	100	Rawlins Real Estate (rent & dep)	$700.00	
5/5	101	County Clerk (fictitious name)	10.00	
5/7	102	The Herald (publishing FNS)	45.00	
5/9	103	Ed's Keyboards (IBM l-mo. & dep)	275.00	
5/9	104	Ed's Keyboards (maint. agreement)	50.00	
5/12	105	Mary Smith (calculator purchase)	25.00	
5/18	106	Telephone Co. (line installation)	150.00	
5/20	107	Phone Store (2-line phone)	79.50	
5/22	108	Ray Brown (logo design)	25.00	
5/24	Cash	The Hungry Dog (lunch/Ray Brown)	6.95	
5/28	109	The Copy Spot (brochures, cards)	118.50	
5/29	110	The Herald (advertising)	370.00	
		Total Expense & Income (May)	**$1,854.95**	**$00.00**

Office Assistance
Cash Journal for June

Date	Check or Invoice #	Detail	(Debit) Expense	(Credit) Income
6/4	111	U.S.P.O. (stamps for mailing)	$29.00	
6/6	112	Office Stationers (supplies, invoices, etc.)	58.90	
6/7	A1	W. Smith		$62.50
6/8	A2	Art Association		112.50
6/9	A3	T. Williams		22.00
6/9	113	Judy Miller (typing fee)	200.00	
6/10	A4	Bank of Cutterville		75.00
6/10	A5	WKTR-FM		120.50
6/13	A6	J. Johnson		43.50
6/15	114	Rawlins Real Estate (rent)	350.00	
6/15	A7	C. Lewis		73.50
6/15	A8	R. Swell		90.00
6/16	115	Judy Miller (typing fee)	200.00	
6/19	A9	W. Smith		52.50
6/23	116	Judy Miller (typing fee)	200.00	
6/26	117	Phone company (bill)	15.90	
6/27	A10	K. Black		48.00
6/30	118	Judy Miller (typing fee)	200.00	
		Total Expense & Income (June)	**$1,253.80**	**$700.00**

Although Bill has only been in business for a month, he is curious about his company's financial worth and decides to work up a balance sheet to get the answer. The calculation, as indicated in the example, is the amount owned (assets) minus the amount due to creditors (liabilities), which equals his worth.

Balance Sheet (as of June 30)

Assets		Liabilities	
Cash on hand & in bank *(Capital balance & June income)*	$6,191.25	Ed's Keyboards *(Balance on IBM)* Unpaid rent *(July)*	$1,725.00 350.00
Office equipment *(Includes full value of IBM even though not paid off)*	2,000.00	Taxes *(estimated)*	75.00
Office furniture	350.00		
Accounts receivable *(Outstanding invoices for work already done)*	400.00	**Liabilities**	$2,150.00
Total Assets	**$8,941.25**	**CAPITAL**	**$6,791.25**
		Total Liabilities	**$8,941.25**

The figure Bill is most interested in is the CAPITAL amount in the Liabilities column. This is the amount remaining after what Bill owes is subtracted from his current assets and is what his business is worth at the end of June. In other words, if he decided to try to sell his business right now, he could realistically ask that amount as a selling price. Of course, Bill probably wouldn't get that amount because he has not yet become established enough to warrant someone buying the business, unless he or she was looking for a "turnkey" operation—in other words, a business to just walk into and get going immediately.

This information is valuable when Bill goes to apply for expansion capital or for credit on future purchases he plans to make. His balance sheet will change each time he prepares it (probably quarterly in the future) as business improves, bringing in greater income and reducing his debts.

In the meantime, the balance sheet gives Bill a tool to use when comparing the financial standing of his business this month against future months and years. It also keeps him current on what he owns, to whom he owes money, and his major sources of income.

The same procedure is used in developing a personal balance sheet, which possibly would be needed to establish credibility when applying for a loan. Assets would include furniture, automobiles, jewelry, a home, and other tangibles, while liabilities would consist of outstanding loans and other major debts.

Bank Statement Reconciliation

Another important step that Bill must handle monthly is reconciling his bank statement against his checkbook register. He simply marks off the checks in his register that have cleared per the bank statement, notes the deposits that have been credited, and deducts any service charges for the previous month from his balance.

Bill then adds up all the outstanding checks—those listed in his register that have not cleared by the closing date indicated on the bank statement—and *deducts* them from the balance indicated on his bank statement. He adds up any deposits that have not yet been credited to his account and then *adds* them to the balance, as follows.

Balance per bank statement	$5,982.15
Plus: Deposits not credited	+325.00
Minus: Outstanding checks	-115.90
New Balance	$ 6,191.25

The new balance figure should match that listed in his checkbook register and, in this case, it does. If, however, the statement and the register did not reconcile, Bill would have a customer representative at the bank review his statement and banking activity for the past month.

Notes

Key Points

_____

_____

_____

_____

_____

_____

Personal Thoughts

_____

_____

_____

_____

_____

Additional Research

_____

_____

_____

_____

_____

_____

16

PRICING FOR PROFITS

One of the toughest problems facing small business owners is establishing prices that the market will bear and that will cover overhead and guarantee a profit.

Often new business owners give the business away to get sales, but this is not an advisable practice. Realistic pricing indicates your confidence in what you are selling, and if you value your service, so will the customer.

Today's consumer realizes that no one gets something worthwhile for nothing, so don't be afraid to establish prices that will work toward your profit goals.

Guidelines

Several factors must be taken into consideration when setting prices:

1. ***The cost of goods sold.*** In the case of a retail or wholesale operation, this is the amount originally paid for the goods. For a manufacturer, it is the cost of producing the goods.

2. ***The nature of the product or service.*** Uniqueness and demand come into play here. In the case of goods with a stable level of demand, such as bread or auto repair, raising or lowering prices will have little effect. However, when demand is high for goods that are hard to get, the price can realistically be set anywhere the business owner wants. Such is often the case with restaurants featuring an exclusive or unusual menu.

3. ***The competition.*** It is important to recognize what your competition is charging, for often this will guide pricing within a certain region. However, if a competitor is charging what you feel is an unrealistic price—either more or less—for a product or service, you owe it to yourself to find out why. Then set your prices according to all of the factors outlined here. Even if your prices are higher than the competitor, consumers will pay the cost if you offer something special, such as a friendly atmosphere, convenient hours, follow-up service or maintenance, or some other benefit not provided by the competition.

4. ***Your company policy.*** This encompasses a number of things, including your location, your position in the marketplace, and additional services offered. It also takes into account your personal philosophy about business and your role in it.

5. ***Market strategy.*** Should you go for large volume at low prices or low volume at high prices? That is the bottom line in considering market strategy. As a small business owner, you will likely opt for low volume and higher prices, since the alternative involves having the resources, including labor, display room, distribution channels, etc., to move large volumes of product or perform major service tasks.

6. ***Customers.*** What will the market bear? In other words, what are your customers willing to pay for your products or services?

People expect prices that are fair; if you are planning to charge overinflated rates you had better be a topnotch salesperson or have something so incredible and unusual to offer that the price won't matter.

Although there are differences between establishing prices for retail operations, wholesale products, manufacturing, and services, the basic formula for price setting is

Labor + Materials + Overhead + Profit Margin = Price

However, before setting prices on goods or services, it is extremely important to understand the concept of the break-even point. Many small business owners operate on an overall profit-loss basis without realizing the importance of cost accounting. Being aware of such factors as your break-even point, markup, and profit margin can tell you which areas of your business are profitable and which are causing a drain.

Understanding Break-even

The break-even point is the minimum amount you must charge in order to cover all expenses incurred for the production and promotion of your goods and/or services *without losing or making money.* In other words, any income that is above the break-even point is considered to be profit and anything below it is a loss.

To find your break-even point, you must first total all of your operating costs, including materials and labor, equipment lease or purchase payments, advertising, utilities, office supplies, and any incidentals such as gasoline, maintenance, and postage.

Generally, this is computed for a particular period of time, such as six months or a year. However, if your business is still in the early stages of operation, you can use the estimated figures on your projected expenses statement and guesstimate costs for materials and labor.

For example, the monthly expenses for your hypothetical cake-decorating business total $300. You want to know what the break-even point would be if you sold an average of 20 cakes per month. The calculation is as follows:

$$\frac{\$300 \text{ (expenses)}}{20 \text{ cakes}} = \$15$$

In order to break even, that is, to operate without losing money or realizing a profit, you must charge a minimum of $15 for each cake sold.

The same process can be used to analyze the break-even point on a weekly basis. First you determine your annual expenses by multiplying the $300 by 12 months, which would give you $3,600 per year.

The calculation to find the weekly break-even point follows:

$$\frac{\$3,600 \text{ (expenses)}}{52 \text{ weeks}} = \$69.23$$

Therefore, you must earn $69.23 per week to operate the business without losing money and without realizing a profit.

Stay Informed

Knowing your break-even point is one of the greatest favors you can do for yourself as a business owner. It tells you how much you must charge for your products or services and is invaluable in setting prices to realize a profit.

Keep in mind, however, that the break-even point is a variable figure. Since it depends on production and overhead costs, plan to reevaluate periodically to make sure your prices reflect any changes.

Labor Costs

Labor costs, obviously, are the expenses incurred for the actual work done to manufacture or sell a product or to perform a service. Think of them as wages or salaries.

Small business owners often end up working for free because they fail to set a wage for themselves. Despite the fact that you will want to reinvest all of the income received back into the business for a while, it is imperative that you establish a fixed salary amount for yourself when figuring operating expenses.

If you have set aside a survival fund to carry you through the first six months of operation, you may want to defer your salary until the business becomes solvent; however, you should still figure the amount into your expenses. Otherwise, you may find the prices you set are too low to justify making a profit from the onset.

It is much easier to set realistic prices from the beginning than it is to raise them later in an attempt to make up the difference. Remember, your time and skills are the cornerstone of your business, so think of paying yourself as you would any valuable employee.

Setting Retail Prices

If you are manufacturing items to sell at retail prices, without using a middleman, use the following formula as a starting point when establishing a selling price for your inventory of goods.

$$\frac{1}{3} \text{ Labor} + \frac{1}{3} \begin{array}{c} \text{Materials} \\ \text{\& Overhead} \end{array} + \frac{1}{3} \text{ Profit} = \begin{array}{c} \text{Selling} \\ \text{Price} \end{array}$$

You need a foundation. One place to start is with your labor costs. If, for example, the monetary value of your time and effort (labor) in producing an item was $6, you would allocate $6 for material, $6 for overhead and an additional $6 as profit for a total selling price of $18.

If materials and overhead are costing more, you can (a) boost the price accordingly; (b) review your expenses and find ways to cut back on material costs, such as finding a less expensive supplier; or (c) utilize a portion of the profit margin to cover the balance. Of the three options, (b) is the best way to go.

You must also keep in mind that when you are producing mass quantities of an item, your costs will be reduced because of price breaks on supplies and reduced labor costs per unit. You are then able to structure your selling price according to previously mentioned pricing factors, such as competition and demand for the product.

If you are starting a retail business that relies on selling products you purchase wholesale, you may have some of your prices set for you by what the competition is doing, or by recommendations made by the wholesaler. However, there will still be items you must price yourself.

Money is the sixth sense which makes it possible for us to enjoy the other five senses.

Richard Ney

This will involve understanding the principle of markup or gross margin—the difference between the cost of goods sold and the selling price, taking into consideration sale markdowns, shortages, and discounts to employees. Generally, markup is stated as a percentage of retail price.

For example, if a manufacturer sells dresses to you at a wholesale price of $12.50 each and you sell them for $25, you would have a 100 percent markup (a 50 percent gross margin).

If you know the cost of goods and the average amount of markup you need to operate profitably, it is relatively simple to determine a price by using the following formula:

$$\frac{\text{Cost of goods}}{100 - \text{markup \%} \times 100} = \text{Retail Price}$$

For example, if you purchased a gross of rubber ducks for a total price of $172.80 and had determined that you needed a gross margin of 36 percent to operate profitably, you would calculate the expected profit as follows:

$$\frac{\$172.80}{100 - 36 \times 100} = \$270$$

When you divide the retail price ($270) by the number of items in a gross (12 dozen or 144 things) you get a unit price of $1.88, which you would probably raise to $1.98, depending on the market, to improve the profit margin slightly and provide leeway for markdowns during sales, etc.

Specialty items, such as antiques, artwork, imported goods, and handcrafted items can be priced higher according to current value and what the market in your area will bear. Their markup usually ranges between 200 and 300 percent.

Setting Wholesale Prices

Operating as a wholesale manufacturer greatly reduces your selling and administrative costs, because you are passing your products on to someone else to sell. Your price to retailers should thus be approximately 50 percent less than the suggested retail price.

In actuality, you are providing retailers with a discount because of their willingness and ability to promote your product.

The formula for wholesale pricing includes your profit margin + labor costs + expenses, which will be appreciably lower than for a retail operation because of savings on advertising, display equipment, and maintenance, but which must include warehousing and marketing.

Pricing is typically more competitive at the wholesale level than at any other and is almost always the determining factor in whether your products are purchased or not.

Also affecting wholesalers are other wholesalers offering competitive pricing, middlemen buying large quantities at low prices, and supply and demand factors.

As a wholesaler, you are in a position to vary prices according to the size of orders and your ability to negotiate with buyers. However, it is a good idea to develop a solid markup base from which to operate. This will allow you the flexibility to offer maximum and minimum prices for each item based on quantity buys.

Pricing is a crucial aspect of managing your business. Since you are in business to make a profit, it is important that you set prices that will result in the greatest income.

Childcare Rates

With your childcare service, obviously, what you charge will directly affect what you earn. The first thing you must ask yourself is what do other providers charge? If you travel around the country, you'll find the range of fee and tuition schedules varies from $50 per week in small towns to $250 or more per week in major metropolitan areas. One exclusive childcare center in New York charges an outrageous $400 per week and has a long waiting list!

Charges are also influenced by such things as the age of the child, the total number of children you can take care of on any given day, your hours of availability (before and after school care, for example), insurance costs and extras you are willing and able to offer, such as hot lunches, extended care and special field trips.

It is important to consider all of these factors when deciding on a fee schedule. You must also determine whether or not to establish a one-time registration fee, late fees when parents do not pick up their children at the arranged time, bad check penalties and charges for extra services.

> *Children stand more in need of example than criticism.*
> Joseph Joubert

Check around your community by looking in the Yellow Pages under "Day Care," "Nursery Schools" or "Child Care" to see what is available. You'll want to investigate these other programs to see what they're offering in the way of services and to find out how much they charge. You can try the straight-forward approach by calling owners and explaining that you are starting a childcare facility and would like information to help you structure your operation in a competitive manner. However, don't expect to always get full cooperation.

One childcare owner told us she found out what her future competitors were doing and charging by calling up as an interested parent and interviewing the owner or manager of several centers on the telephone. The problem with this is they will probably invite you to visit their facility, which will give you a good idea of internal organization; however, they may also want you to bring along the child you say you want to enroll.

So, although this is a relatively good investigative method, it is one that may cause you to compromise yourself, which is not always the best philosophy. It is recommended that you use the more direct approach or talk to mothers of young children in the neighborhood—chances are good that they have an idea of what area childcare centers are charging.

Prices: Fair and Competitive

The fees you eventually set will need to be competitive with those of existing services, though not so low as to affect your projected profit margin. But you wlll find that you can charge more if you can offer a clearly superior program to others in the area.

When you've seen the range of services provided in your community at present, take a look at how your service will be different and more comprehensive. Then take a look at how that margin of higher quality can translate into better profits.

The following sample fee schedule was developed from information we received and averaged out during our interviews with childcare providers across the country. The figures are based on discussions with owner/operators in three small cities with an average population of 500,000 each.

Sample Fee Schedule

Charge Per Month	Age of Child
$120	age 6 and older (before and after school)
$200	age 5 (older children during summer)
$225	ages 4 to 5
$250	ages 2 to 4
$300	ages 1 to 2, or toilet trained
$350	up to age 1

If you want to make, say, $1,000 a month to supplement another income in the family, accepting four children in the two to four age group in your home-based childcare center would give you the income you desire with a high profit margin because of low overhead expenses.

If, however, you are in the market to earn in the upper bracket of the industry, you must expect to set up a facility in a commercial location, such as a renovated house, a storefront with yard space or access to a park or, possibly, a rented room in a church or community center. Then you would be able to take in between twenty to fifty children at a time, which will bring you a higher gross income, but a lower profit margin.

In any event, one of the most important aspects in determining your fees and projected income is to never take in more children than you honestly feel you can handle effectively, with or without extra help. By taking in fewer children, you may be able to charge a premium for your "personalized care" to parents who feel this is an important benefit and, therefore, increase income.

Pricing Considerations

There are a number of variables that should also be considered when setting rates, each of which can affect your fee range:

1. How high is the demand for childcare in your area?
2. What is the general income level of families in your area?
3. Is there a typical "style" of childcare programs in your area?
4. Will you have to purchase additional equipment, or bring your home or commercial location up to a better level of safety and comfort?
5. What are the supplies and items you will need continually and what do they cost?
6. What kinds of foods will you serve for lunches and/or snacks?
7. Will there be transportation costs?
8. Do you need paid help?

9. Will you provide infant supplies and food?

10. Are there insurance costs?

11. Are there license costs?

Other pricing factors to consider are as follows:

♦ **The type of service being provided.** If you are willing to accept a child who requires special attention for any reason, be it dietary or personal care, the parents should be willing to pay extra for your time. This is not unfair or unprofessional; if administering to one child means you must hire additional help or take away from the attention you give the other children, the extra charge is justified.

♦ **Time.** It is not unrealistic to add a premium for parents who consistently expect you to watch their children before or after your normal operating hours. Although the majority of parents will adhere to your rules, you may find that you have one or two who try to bend the rules according to their needs. However, if they understand that you are going to charge them for the luxury, the incidents may be reduced to only those extreme emergencies.

♦ **Budget.** Young single parents, and even two-parent families striving to make ends meet may find themselves in a cash bind now and then. If they have been good paying customers you may want to help them out with a reduced rate now and then as a gesture of good will. Don't make this a habit, however, as everyone will expect the same treatment. Use common sense in establishing fees in these situations.

♦ **Your reputation.** As word of your center spreads, your waiting list will grow appreciably. Some top-rated childcare centers actually sign up babies before they are born! Obviously, when you get to this point, you are justified in raising your rates.

Remember: Unless you are located in an area where childcare facilities are in excessively high demand, it will probably take a while until you are operating at full capacity and able to realize a profit. It is, therefore, vital that you plan ahead and develop a realistic blueprint for growth. The majority of owner/operators we spoke with claim it takes between six and nine months to reach 90 percent capacity.

If Clients Don't Pay

After you've chosen a fee schedule, make sure each parent understands the schedule and when payment is due. Though there may be times you will make exceptions for individual parents, you should have a general payment policy and adhere to it. The bottom line is: You have a business to run, and you can't run it without income.

The majority of parents will pay according to your expectations, partly because it is so difficult to find good childcare. If, however, you run into a slow-pay problem, you have several avenues of recourse.

The first step is to talk with the parent and explain that you cannot keep their child in the center if fees are not paid in a timely manner. State that you realize they may have some financial problem, even if you know they haven't, and that you are willing to work with them on an easy payment schedule, e.g., so much per week versus one lump sum at the end of every month. In other words, give them the benefit of the doubt. In most cases, this will result in immediate payment.

Getting Tough

If that doesn't work, however, you may be forced to expel their child from the program. If the parents still have an outstanding balance with you, try to collect by making a personal visit to their home or office. Explain that you have provided childcare services in good faith and have expenses that must be covered by their payment.

If this doesn't elicit a check or promise of payment in the near future, explain that you will be forced to take further action. If they ask what you intend to do, just say that they will be hearing from you or your representative within a few days, which gives you a chance to figure out what the next step will be.

Ask your lawyer to send a standard collection letter on his or her letterhead. Often this tactic will be just the fuel needed to spark them into writing a check. It will cost you—probably your attorney's hourly charge—but is worth it if the bill is substantial.

Last Resorts

Small claims court is another option. Although it takes time, it is inexpensive. Claims are limited to debts up to a certain amount (anywhere from $1,200 to $2,000 depending on your state). There are two things to keep in mind when taking someone to small claims court.

One: The judgment may not be made in your favor depending on how the judge weighs both sides of the story, which means you lose the amount due as well as the time and money invested in filing the claim.

Two: Even if a judgment is made in your favor, it doesn't guarantee that you will receive payment immediately if the client still decides to hold back or claims that they are under financial duress.

Collection agencies take a percentage, and it can be a large one, of the final amount collected as payment. Basically they hound the client and send nasty letters indicating how their credit rating is going to be affected by not paying your bill. Sometimes it works and sometimes it doesn't.

Creative collecting has proven successful for many people. One owner, who was owed three months worth of fees for child-care, told us how she called every other day-care center in the area until she found out where the delinquent parent had enrolled his child.

She informed the owner of that service about the bad debt and suggested they get a "deposit" based on the parent's record. Within two weeks, the parent sent a check for the full amount with an apology based, she felt, on his embarrassment. Although this and other creative methods might not always work, for example, if the family moves away, it can be worth the time and effort if it results in payment.

Notes

Key Points

_____

_____

_____

_____

_____

_____

Personal Thoughts

_____

_____

_____

_____

_____

_____

Additional Research

_____

_____

_____

_____

_____

_____

17

INVENTORY AS INVESTMENT

Ask 100 small business owners what inventory means to them and more than 90 percent will tell you it's the merchandise they keep on hand to sell to their customers, or the materials and supplies stocked to produce goods or perform a service.

This is somewhat accurate, for inventory can and should be viewed as any supplies, raw materials, or finished goods used to generate a profit in your business. But it isn't the response that a savvy business owner would give.

Surprisingly, according to a recent study conducted by a leading consulting firm, less than 10 percent of a group of 500 entrepreneurs interviewed spoke of their inventory in terms of the *investment it represents;* an investment that can range from 15 to 25 percent of total operating capital.

It is because of this misunderstanding that many small business owners often fail to incorporate good inventory control practices into their regular management routine. Although they keep an eagle eye on every penny going through the books, they may totally overlook the cash tied up in their inventory.

Controlling Inventory

Inventory control can be a very simple, straightforward task if you implement a workable system from the beginning—preferably even *before* you start ordering and receiving goods. You will find that time really flies when you are self-employed, and it's very easy to postpone such tasks as inventory control until the inevitable day you find yourself facing this overwhelming job. Inventory control will give you valuable information about: (a) whether or not you are carrying too much or too little inventory based on, for example, items and prices preferred by your customers, or seasonal aspects, and (b) if you are realizing optimum economy determined by the costs of storage, taxes, handling, and the investment per unit.

The ideal situation is to maintain an inventory that is profitable because it turns over (comes in and goes out of the business) regularly, thereby lowering the cost of storing, displaying, and insuring it.

There are several methods of inventory control that you can adopt, depending on your business. The main goal with each method, however, is to tell you how many items you have on hand and how many you need to meet your customer or production demands. It will also work toward lessening inventory shrinkage, which is generally the result of employee pilferage; customer theft; incorrect inventory storage; or sloppy record maintenance of items ordered, received, and used.

You can tell how many items you currently have by making an educated guess, which generally only works for businesses having a small, visible inventory that is relatively predictable. An example of the kind the business that could probably operate efficiently with this relaxed form of inventory control would be a one- or two-person enterprise that monthly goes through a box of invoices and similar supplies available for a minimum amount at the discount office-supply store.

Other methods of inventory control are *the physical count,* which should be done at least once a year for tax purposes, or—the easiest and most efficient of them all—*an ongoing* record. Ideally, you should incorporate both systems by backing up periodic physical counts with a perpetual record.

To set up your perpetual system, simply create a file card or inventory sheet in a three-ring binder for each item in your inventory. Across the top of the card or sheet, list the following:

1. Item name and code number, if applicable
2. A description of the item
3. Where it is stored
4. The supplier's name, address, and phone number
5. Unit price (i.e., $12.95/dozen)
6. Your selling price if a retail item, or percentage of gross price of completed product, if used for manufacturing or service
7. The date you place an order
8. The number of items and the date they are received

Then, every time you sell or use an item, write it down and subtract it from the last balance. You should also indicate the reorder number, based on when and by how much you must replenish your stock.

The reorder number will be determined by such factors as the following:

1. The minimum cost per unit available from your supplier, including quantity discounts, preseason specials, and discounts for cash or quick payment
2. The delivery schedule—the delay between placing the order and receiving it
3. Economic and social trends that can affect the way an item is perceived by the public

For example, during a depressed or inflated economy, sales for leisure or discretionary items typically drop. By keeping an eye on these factors, you can adjust your inventory needs accordingly and not get stuck with great quantities of items that you can't move.

After a while, you will be able to recognize at a glance which items are movers and which are simply taking up shelf space. When you reach this point, your ordering skills will become much more efficient and your investment in inventory will become a profitable proposition.

Notes

Key Points
_____

_____

_____

_____

_____

_____

_____

Personal Thoughts
_____

_____

_____

_____

_____

_____

Additional Research
_____

_____

_____

_____

_____

_____

18

MAKING THE MOST OF YOUR TIME

$\mathbf{A}$ recent survey of small business owners indicated that one of the qualities they felt contributed the most to their success was organization. In conjunction with this is the fact that time management and basic organizational seminars continue to be the most popular offerings in adult education catalogs and business workshops around the country.

Time is money! It is vital to your success that you learn to manage your time and organize paperwork. This might sound rather simplistic, but you would be amazed at the number of small business owners who operate in a constant state of chaos.

Although we have seen a number of "A messy office is the sign of a creative mind" posters on entrepreneurs' office walls, it is a good bet that the holders of these signs can recount story after story of missing checks, lost orders, or misplaced files, which disrupted or halted the flow of business until they were located.

The survey respondents also stated that once they had learned to manage their time in both their personal and business lives and had set up guidelines for handling routine tasks, they felt more confident about accepting new challenges and making decisions.

The simple truth about getting organized is that it clears your mind for taking care of the nitty-gritty, profit-making aspects of being in business—production and promotion. For example, just by setting aside a certain place in your work area to hold customer files and billing information, you have made one major step toward maximizing production. Knowing that all the supplies and materials needed to conduct your business are located in one place saves you both time and energy.

Making Time Work for You

Time management is the ability to take the hours we have available and use them to our advantage. Making lists of tasks to be done and giving them a priority rating is one of the best ways to avoid losing precious moments.

Keep a monthly calendar handy to help you keep track of major commitments, important dates, and appointments. Try to avoid using it for notations of daily work in progress, carryover tasks, or other things that are best suited for inclusion on your daily and weekly lists. There are several other ideas you can easily incorporate into your working lifestyle that will maximize your productivity.

Work Smart

Handle the jobs you find most difficult or cumbersome during peak performance time. If you are a morning person and find that making telephone calls to potential customers is one of your least favorite tasks, make those calls first thing in the morning when you are feeling fresh and energetic. Then organize the rest of the day's tasks accordingly.

Set Realistic Daily Goals for Yourself

Just because you are the key employee, don't try to do everything at once. Learn just how much work you can accept and expect to accomplish in a given period of time and allow yourself to turn down work if it seems like it will be too much for you to handle.

Positive Reinforcement

When you work alone, as many small business owners do when getting their businesses off the ground, there generally aren't many people around to support or praise your work...and everyone needs strokes! Remember that a customer's praises are proof that you are doing a good job.

Reward Yourself

Sometimes it is easy to forget that you are important to the business—you *are* the business. So treat yourself to a special dinner now and then or plan an evening where you go out to a movie or do something else that has absolutely nothing to do with business. Remind yourself that this is your reward for accomplishing certain goals for your business. It will help to keep your spirits high.

Don't Procrastinate

Don't put off doing tasks that must be done. If you constantly let some tasks slide because you don't enjoy doing them or they are boring and time-consuming, you will soon find yourself back-logged and unable to catch up. The effects of procrastination may not be obvious until you are faced with a deadline and, at that point, you will realize that you are working at less than maximum efficiency using the wrong supplies, feeling tense, and being hassled by minor problems that could have been avoided. Even when business is slow and it seems that there could be little harm done by taking a day off to go to the beach, be sure to complete all your required tasks before closing up shop.

Limit Personal Phone Calls

Ask friends and relatives not to call during established business hours. These friendly calls not only eat into productive time, they tie up the line when an important client may be trying to get in touch with you. The same holds true with visitors. If you are self-employed, friends and family often feel that you are not really "working" and that they can stop by anytime to chat. Explain that you will be happy to visit with them at some other time and be sure to tell them why so there aren't any ill feelings.

Obviously, there will be times when unavoidable situations arise, such as an emergency or an unexpected problem. Take these into consideration by estimating how long a project will take and then adding a bit of extra time to give yourself some leeway.

Delegate

If you find that you absolutely cannot handle a certain aspect of the business, such as your own bookkeeping, for example, don't labor over the task—you will end up wasting a great deal of time and could make some serious mistakes. Admit to yourself that the task is just not your strong point and make arrangements to have someone else do it.

Learn to Say "No"

One of the hardest things for most people to do is to say "no." Even when we realize that helping a friend out on a special project will cost valuable time, we often agree to do it because we hate to say no. What we do is justify our acceptance by assuring ourselves that saying yes will put us in the position of meeting a lot of potential customers. The reality is that using that time to make phone calls or a sales call for your own business will probably result in a paying customer, not just a potential contact.

Minimize Business Meetings

Before setting up a formal meeting, which can be very time-consuming, see if you can take care of the matter by phone or through the mail. If a meeting can't be avoided, make sure you specify a time limit to encourage people to get down to business. Another time-saving device for meetings is to work up an agenda that outlines exactly what has to be discussed to avoid idle chit-chat and unnecessary diversions.

Plan Your Time

When you have to run errands, plan them for a sensible time, such as in the morning when traffic is light. Plan to do as many things as possible in one trip, outlining the stops you must make so they follow a sequential order.

Notes

Key Points

_____

_____

_____

_____

_____

_____

Personal Thoughts

_____

_____

_____

_____

_____

Additional Research

_____

_____

_____

_____

_____

19

Hiring Employees

One of the benefits of starting small is that you don't have to hire anyone to work for you. As the demand for your service grows and you enroll more children, however, you will probably need to have some help, at least on a part-time basis. If possible, hire assistants as independent contractors to start with; that means they take care of their own insurance and taxes.

There are regulatory guidelines that tell you how you need to staff based on how many and the ages of the children you care for. Obviously, a low child/staff ratio is better because the children get more focused attention.

While you need to check with state and local agencies for specific requirements, here are some recommended ratios:

♦ One caregiver for every three children one year old or less

♦ One caregiver for every four to five children aged one to two

♦ One caregiver for every six children aged two to three

Ideal ratios depend on the caregiver's ability to work with a certain number of children and still be able to give the attention and care that are necessary.

In terms of what you pay your help, you will need to see how other local services recruit and compensate staff. If you have a small, home-based business, you will not be able to provide a comprehensive salary and benefits package. Most likely, you will want to find students from a local high school or university who are studying education or child development and need practical experience, and are willing to work for close to minimum wage.

Another wonderful option is to hire retirees who are looking for a way to supplement their income. They generally have excellent experience and will provide the children with a solid sense of security and "grandparenting."

> *There's a big difference between busy and real work.*
>
> Anonymous

Just make sure you are complying with all applicable regulations when hiring help, and be sure you know what income tax needs are required.

As soon as you feel you are ready, place an ad in the classified section of the local newspaper to recruit potential workers. Also register with your state unemployment office. Students, who will only be available on a seasonal basis but are generally good workers, can be found by contacting placement offices at major colleges and universities. Retirees may be recruited through the ad or by contacting senior citizen residences in your area. In addition, you can often find qualified people in friends or family members of current employees.

Interested applicants should fill out a standard employment application (available in any stationery store) and provide references from former employers. Check these references very carefully to find out about the applicant's sense of loyalty, responsibility, and honesty, as well as their history working with children.

Selection of Candidates

Be prepared to screen quite a few people who are just looking for interim employment or who just don't fit what you're looking for. It takes time to find good workers who are willing to make a commitment to the job. You don't want to waste time training people who are not going to stay.

The Interview Process

Schedule a personal interview to make your own determination based on poise, appearance, level of interest in the job, abilities, and future goals. Write out interview questions ahead of time to help you stay on track.

Set up the interview in a comfortable place to put the candidate at ease. For example, if you operate out of your home, you may want to arrange to meet in a nearby coffee shop during a slow time, or if you have an office, set it up when you won't be interrupted by phone calls or clients.

In addition to finding out about the candidate's capabilities and goals, you will want to use this time to talk about the company, your expectations, the work standards, and, of course, the pay structure. Explain that the work may be sporadic and, if this doesn't seem to present a problem to the applicant, add his or her name to your roster of employees to call when needed.

On-the-Job Training

When you find someone who seems to have all the qualifications needed, arrange to train him or her on the job. Many owners like to do this themselves, to ensure that their standards are instilled from the beginning and to get a first-hand idea of the new recruit's work habits. If you have a trusted employee, have the new recruit accompany your staffer on assignments to learn the ropes. (This extra duty should always result in a bonus for the employee doing the training.)

Training may take several days or weeks, depending on the worker's previous experience. Basically, a good training process should involve the following steps:

1. Gain the recruit's confidence by putting him or her at ease.

2. Find out what he or she already knows.

3. Indicate the importance of the specific task being taught.

4. Explain and demonstrate each step patiently.

5. Be sure each step is understood before moving on to the next.

6. Encourage and welcome questions.

7. Have the recruit try to do the task.

8. Correct mistakes gently.

9. Have him or her repeat the steps for you.

10. When you are both comfortable, let the recruit go out on his or her own.

11. Review performance periodically.

12. Offer support by letting the employee train others when ready.

Taking time to train properly reduces turnover and accidents, improves the quality of work performed, lowers your cost of labor, and increases productivity. Every time you have to replace an employee and train a new one, you're losing productivity.

Overtraining the Ambitious

Sometimes it is possible to train people so well they feel they can start their own business in competition with yours. This can occur when an employee realizes you are making money off his or her hard work. There are several ways to stay on top of your employees' activities.

If you're sure an employee is thinking of starting a business, take him or her aside and explain the administrative aspects of the business. Find out if he or she truly realizes that you are providing steady work on a regular basis and if it's really clear how much is involved in running a business.

In rare cases, you are going to lose an employee who feels confident enough to start a business, and there isn't too much you can do about it.

In other situations, you can promote the employee as appropriate. This is feasible only if your cash flow and the employee's ability warrant it.

The Benefits of Happy Employees

Personnel management is a time-consuming job for the business owner. However, paying attention to the needs of your employees and working to gain their trust and maintain their loyalty can do nothing but benefit your business.

The attitude of your employees about your management techniques plays an important part in building and maintaining your reputation in the business world. If employees are treated fairly and with respect, their job satisfaction will be reflected in the way they do their jobs.

This is something that can truly keep you ahead of the competition; a loyal, efficient, and enthusiastic group of workers is one of your most effective forms of public relations, so never scrimp when it comes to keeping your employees happy. A few important rules of thumb in dealing with employees include the following:

♦ **Never expect an employee to do something you wouldn't do.** This is why training new recruits yourself is such a good idea; it shows them that you are willing and able to step in and do anything that needs to be done.

♦ **Listen to your employees.** Talk to your staff regularly and incorporate any ideas they have whenever feasible. Remember that they have firsthand knowledge about how certain aspects of the job are done and might know if they can be done more efficiently. Suggestions that work for the good of the company should be rewarded with a bonus.

♦ **Take the time to talk about business standards and practices.** Make sure everyone knows exactly what is expected of them. Outline duties and responsibilities on the job and schedule regular reviews to ensure that they are constantly met. If you find it necessary to talk to an employee about work habits, do it in private. And do not criticize; offer constructive ways that performance can be improved.

♦ **Treat each employee as an individual.** When someone seems to be having personal problems that are interfering with his or her work, be willing to allow him or her time off without penalty to take care of the situation. An employee plagued with problems may carry them to work, and this could have a negative effect on productivity. It is much better to get someone to fill in until the regular employee is operating at full efficiency again.

Notes

Key Points

_____

_____

_____

_____

_____

_____

_____

Personal Thoughts

_____

_____

_____

_____

_____

Additional Research

_____

_____

_____

_____

_____

_____

20

ADVERTISING YOUR BUSINESS

More than 150 years ago, Thomas Macaulay, a British historian and statesman, said, "Advertising is to business what steam is to industry. [They provide] the same propelling power."

Few in business would argue with Macaulay's observation—it is as true today as it was when steam was the driving force behind industry. But the question remains, "How do you get the most out of your advertising dollar?" The answer is to

1. Know your customer
2. Target your market
3. Understand the basics of advertising

In this chapter, we will provide an overview of various aspects of advertising, including how to use circulation figures to figure your cost per thousand (CPM) and how to create ads that will bring results.

What Is Advertising?

Advertising informs the public about

♦ Who you are

♦ What kind of business you operate

♦ How they can buy your services

♦ Why they should come to you

Before you even open the doors of your business, you should start thinking about your advertising program—how much money you can afford to spend, where your dollars will be best spent, and how to structure your campaign.

Decide what kind of results you want. Are you looking for immediate enrollment or ongoing recognition? What kind of clients are you hoping to attract? Are you emphasizing price, service, or something unique? Once you have answered these questions, your decision as to the best type of advertising for the allotted dollars will be easier to make.

There are three basic types of advertising that you will be most interested in during the first few years of your business.

Start-up Advertising

This includes your business cards and stationery, announcement flyers, and brochures, and your initial ads in newspapers or other publications. At this point, your main focus will be on telling people where you are located and what you can offer them.

Ongoing Advertising

Once the business is up and running, it will be vital to your success to institute a regular advertising campaign that is well thought out and—this is the key—consistent. Your goal at this point is to attract new clients, obtain repeat business from existing clients, and enhance your reputation.

Appearance Advertising

After you have reached the point where your business is on steady ground and you're showing increased profits every year, you can afford to dabble in "institutional advertising," as it is called in the trade. This is where you pick up the tab to send a dozen kids to the rodeo when it comes to town, or you sponsor a float in the local parade and, in return, get your name listed on the program or on a banner in the parade. This is primarily name recognition only and, while every little bit is helpful, by the time you can afford it, you probably will be in pretty good shape anyway.

Reaching a Specialized Market

Once you've determined the service you'll be offering, you need to reach your market. If you're planning to specialize, the people who will be using your services will be easy to identify. You'll most likely be able to reach them easily through a mailing and a follow-up call.

You can buy targeted mailing lists from a list broker or you can simply go through the Yellow Pages and create a mailing list. If, for example, you're planning on specializing in legal word processing, such as transcribing attorneys' case notes, your list should include every attorney's office within a twenty-mile radius.

Design a simple letter or flyer that outlines your background and abilities. Build your mailing list on one of the database-management programs and type the names and addresses on the blank section of the flyer. Then simply staple a business card to each and send them off.

Best Bets for Your Childcare Business

There are many types of advertising media that will give you the local exposure you want: flyers, newspapers, magazines, radio, television, Yellow Pages, handbills, and so on. Some sources cost a considerable amount of money, others cost little more than the price of photocopies and time.

Before you commit financial resources to paid advertising, see how much business you get by means of cards and notices on

Sample Flyer

LOVING CHILDCARE

Your Child is Our Top Priority

We Happily Take Care of
Your Little One While You:

WORK

HAVE LUNCH

RUN ERRANDS

GO SHOPPING

MEET FRIENDS

ATTEND A MEETING

TAKE IN A LECTURE

READ A BOOK

Ages 2 to 6
Short-Term Drop In
Full Day and Extended Care
Licensed and Registered

Call for a Free Consultation
555-5555

bulletin boards at the laundromat, grocery store, video store, church, wherever. Think about where you want to focus your efforts, and put up notices in areas where they are apt to be noticed by the people you want to reach.

Another good way to spend advertising dollars (when you are just starting out) is to order business cards. For about $20 you can order 500 business cards after designing your own unique logo with your computer system and graphics software. These cards will reach a great many potential customers if you hand them out freely.

Your choices for electronic media are television and radio. The cost for air time varies widely with different markets. Contact the radio and TV stations in your area and ask what they charge, and if they offer creative services (ad writing) as well.

Options for printed media are *classified* and *display* advertisements. Classified ads generally run a few lines, are not too expensive, and will draw potential customers who are specifically looking for a service such as yours. Display ads, on the other hand, offer more visual information, and are more likely to be seen by people as they browse through a publication. As mentioned in the chapter on marketing, place your ads in targeted media. There are subject- or industry-specific publications on almost every subject.

A display ad would attempt to make more individual contact with the prospective customer. Browse through the local newspapers or a DTP magazine, and see how other people create their display ads. This will give you ideas for your own ads.

When you find an ad that works, stick with it. As they say, "If it's not broken, don't fix it."

Classified Advertising

Classified ads can be crucial to business revenue—an inexpensive way to sell your service and hire employees. Don't underestimate the power of classified ads. Many major corporations use the classifieds even though they have sizable budgets available for display advertising. There are several reasons for this.

1. The classifieds are an extremely reliable testing ground for new products, services, and ideas. Although it is true

that people who typically read the classifieds are a different group from those who scan display ads, they are considered to be responsive and, therefore, can give you a very good idea of whether or not you have placed your ad in the appropriate publication.

2. A short, well-written classified placed in the right publication and under the proper category can be a low-cost method of advertising that guarantees solid returns.

3. If a company is trying to establish a mailing list, a classified ad that features an "Inquiry" statement, such as "Send name and address for free details (or a brochure)," is a good way to build up a file of qualified buyers' names. And they can be considered qualified buyers because it takes time, energy, and the cost of a postage stamp for them to get your free information. By writing to you they have stated their interest.

4. Classified ads are inexpensive, ranging from 50¢ to $15 per word, depending on the publication. With careful planning, you should be able to get broad-based coverage without putting a dent in your operating capital.

Sample Classified Advertisements:

LOVING CHILDCARE: Personalized service at a reasonable price. Full-time or short-term care. Ages 2 to 6. Call today 555-5555 for a free consultation.

INFANTS OUR SPECIALITY: We believe that education should start early. While you are at work, we offer a series of proven techniques to give your child a head start. Call LOVING CHILDCARE today for a free tour and consultation. 555-5555.

Display Advertising

Don't dismiss the possibility of running small display ads on a seasonal basis, even though they are more expensive than classified advertising. Focus on promoting through display advertising during specific times of the year when you know that certain markets will need them.

Choose your publications wisely, concentrating on related trade publications. Consider offering an incentive, such as a 10 percent discount if customers bring in the ad. This will help you track responses and plan future display ad campaigns.

As with all types of advertising, it is important to define your market when getting ready to place a display ad. Your main goal is to select a publication that will reach the audience you want, then create a specific, attention-getting ad that appeals to that target group.

To Write or Not to Write

Writing display ad copy is not for the inexperienced. Although it is possible to learn how to put ideas and words together that will pull the results you desire, it is recommended that you hire a copywriter if you have any qualms about producing an ad.

However, if you are confident that you can develop your own ad, remember that it must build identity through the use of carefully planned words and design. Glance through newspapers and magazines to find ads that catch your eye. Most likely, the ones that stand out have a memorable logo, effective use of space, or an unusual headline that leads you into the body of the ad.

These are ads you should refer to as samples when designing your own.

When planning your ad, keep the following elements in mind:

1. *Visibility.* Your ad may be surrounded by many others, so design it so that it will immediately attract the reader's attention.

2. *Boldness.* Use large art and/or a bold headline as a focal point.

3. **Simplicity.** Don't overwhelm the reader with too many fine details. The ad's main point is lost and so is the reader's attention. This is particularly true in a small ad.

4. **White space.** Just because you have, say, a four-by-six-inch space to work with, it isn't necessary to fill it up. In fact, white space is a necessary component in assuring your ad will be read.

5. **Use simple-to-read typefaces.** Two that are popular are Times Roman and Bookman, which are known as serif typefaces because of the tiny strokes at the tops and bottoms of the letters.

    Sans-serif (without strokes) typefaces, such as Helvetica, are fine for ads containing only a few words, but are difficult for the eye to follow when there is a lot of text.

    Also, be sure that the type is large enough; generally nothing smaller than 10-point type should be used. If type is too small to read, it will simply be ignored.

Design and Typesetting

It isn't necessary to be a great artist to create an ad, especially these days with the availability of a variety of impressive graphic software programs. In addition, you can buy cut-out-and-transfer (press-on) letters in different typefaces, symbols, borders, and designs through graphic art supply companies. Most word processing programs also contain computer graphics that can dress up your ad at a low cost.

If you feel uncomfortable about laying out your ad so it has eye appeal, consider hiring an art student to handle the job for a prearranged fee or as a school assignment. (Talk with the head of the art department to see if there is a work/study for credit program.) Just be sure to review the student's work prior to making a commitment.

Also, check with the advertising department of the newspaper or magazine you are planning to advertise in. There may be graphic artists or designers on staff who will work on the layout

Sample Display Advertisement

Working 9 to 5?
Luncheon Date?
Errands to Run?

• Licensed & Registered
• Ages 2 to 6
• Short Notice Drop-Off
• Full-Day 7:00 a.m.
to 6:00 p.m.
• Indoor/Outdoor Creative Play

Bring the kids to

Loving Childcare

Better babysitting at a better price!

Call us today for a free consultation.

123 E. Main Street.

555-5555

for you. In fact, there are still newspapers in the country that offer full service, from ad concept to design work, at a minimal charge to their advertising clients.

Publications work on tight deadlines, so be sure you start the process early enough to get a proof copy of your ad back in time to make any corrections. You can imagine the anguish in seeing your ad appear with the wrong address. Although the publication would probably do a "make-good" for you and run a corrected ad at no charge, the damage has already been done. The final responsibility for the ad rests with you, so, as with any other aspect of your business, plan ahead.

Tracking Ad Response

Some customers will tell you that they saw your ad and might even let you know what they liked or disliked about it if you ask them. Even so, you should develop other methods for determining if your advertising is working.

One very simple way is to include a coupon for something in the ad and then count the number of coupons you get within a certain test period after the ad runs. There is one major problem with this, however. Even the most well-intentioned people often cut coupons, file them away in a "safe" place, and totally forget about them.

So, although you will be able to gauge response to some degree, be aware that many of the people who come into or call your business have probably seen the coupon but simply mislaid it or are not the kind of folks who use them.

> *Advertising is the greatest art form of the twentieth century.*
> *Marshall McLuhan*

Predicting Ad Response

There is a standardized formula in advertising that provides a barometer for predicting how much response can be expected from either a display ad or a classified ad. The formula states that you will see one-half of the total responses from an ad within a certain period of time after receiving your first inquiry or order.

For an ad run in a daily newspaper, the period of time is three days; for a weekly newspaper or magazine, it is six days; within fifteen days for a monthly publication, and within twenty-five days when running in a bimonthly. Although there will be exceptions to this rule, it does give you a base from which to track response.

Determining Your Cost Per Thousand

The cost per thousand (CPM) equation helps you develop a cost-effective campaign. Basically, it tells you what your ad cost per thousand readers will be. Most publications will provide a CPM comparison upon request (some include it in their Media Kits), but you can figure it out for yourself with just a few facts from publications that you are exploring as advertising vehicles.

For convenience sake, CPM equations are typically based on the rate of a full-page, black-and-white ad. You simply divide the full-page rate by the thousands of circulation. It is important that you get the circulation, *not* the readership, because magazines and newspapers typically claim that their readership is 2 to 50 percent higher because of "pass-along" of the publication to friends or relatives.

For example, if a certain newspaper is charging $2,000 for a full-page ad, and it claims the true circulation is 200,000, you will be paying $10 per 1,000 readers for your ad space. Another specialized publication's full-page rate may be $1,000 with a circulation of 50,000. The cost per 1,000 readers will be much higher–$20 per 1,000, but it might be worth it if, for example, you have a unique product or service that is geared to an exclusive market.

Benefits of Paid Circulation

It is also important to know that publications with a paid circulation generally have a readership that is more inclined to respond to advertising. This is because of the simple fact that they are a captive audience who have taken the time to *order* the publication. This is especially valuable if you have a product or service that you're planning to market through mail-order channels.

You can find circulation, readership demographics, advertising rates, and other important information about a number of publications (especially those with national distribution) through *Standard Rate and Data Service (SRDS)*, available through the research desk of your local library.

The Advertising Research Foundation and the Association of Business Publishers conducted a study to determine the impact of advertising on the sale of products. Several different products were used for the study, and each was advertised for a twelve-month period in an appropriate publication. The results were interesting, but not surprising to anyone who has ever utilized a solid advertising campaign in promoting a business.

♦ More advertising meant more sales.

♦ Determining results from an ad campaign generally took four to six months. One or two insertions do not indicate viable results.

♦ Color in advertisements dramatically increased response and sales.

♦ A well-developed ad campaign keeps on working for a year and sometimes even longer in publications with high "keep" appeal.

Direct Mail

Another way to target specific markets is through direct mail using brochures, flyers, and other materials outlining your childcare business and detailing the benefits of using your services. You get direct-mail pieces all the time. All of those catalogs, brochures, or other solicitation materials you get in the mail from people you've never contacted are direct mail.

Since you haven't requested this information, you may throw it away without a second glance. However, if it's an attractive or unusual advertising piece, you probably decide to look it over. Maybe something—a picture or catchy copy—grabs your eye and you order a product from the company that mailed the material.

These days direct mail is a more expensive proposition because of postage, but if you mail only to select groups or ZIP codes within your city to pull the best response, it can be worthwhile.

Mailing lists can be compiled as you gather names, or you can rent/buy them. Mailing lists, broken down by ZIP codes, income brackets, and other specific factors, are available from some printers and small print shops as well as from advertising agencies, local publications, and mailing-list brokers. Check in the library for a *Direct Mail List Rate and Data* volume to find brokers in the areas you desire. You may not even need to rent a list. The phone book is an excellent source for compiling a mailing list. If you want to get into producing newsletters for business and industry, for example, look in the Yellow Pages and make a list of all the businesses you'd like to approach. The same applies to any other segment of the population you'd like to market your services to.

If you do institute a direct-mail program, be sure to send regular announcements to those who have responded to ads in the past but didn't use your service. Circumstances frequently change, and sending reminders that you are still in business offering quality service at a fair price is sure to result in a response at some point.

Just be aware that the average return for direct mail is between 1 and 2.5 percent, so don't expect the phone to ring off the hook every time you send a mailing. Consistency is the important factor here.

There are advantages to using direct mail when starting out, though the cost is too high for most people to use it right off. The primary benefit is control. You can rent a mailing list that is made up of the names and addresses of very specific groups of people.

When you decided on the type of childcare services you plan on providing, you probably had an idea about your ideal client population. Obviously, if you can reach these potential clients in a focused manner, you will have a greater percentage of people reading your ad materials than if you use general mass advertising.

Designing Your Package

What goes into the direct-mail package? A letter that is both a handshake to introduce yourself and a sales presentation. It can be a tough balance. Sales letters are the least expensive direct-mail pieces to produce, but they are far from the easiest to write. You may want to hire a copywriter to handle that task for best results. If you choose to write the letter yourself, bear in mind these points:

♦ The letter introduces your service to potential buyers.

♦ A dynamic lead-in sentence is essential.

♦ The benefits of dealing with you must be concise and clear.

♦ There should be a feeling of personal communication to the person who's reading it.

♦ It must be highly professional.

Think of what it takes to draw you into a direct-mail piece and keep you interested until the last word: a thought-provoking phrase in big, bold letters at the top of the page; a simple but thorough explanation of why the letter was being sent and how reading it would be of benefit to you; a direct request to take action; a few testimonials from the service's users; the signature of the company's president. All these factors should be considered when preparing your direct-mail sales letter.

Experiment with writing a letter, get some feedback from friends and associates—perhaps even test it locally—but make sure you're sending out something you truly believe will work for you. Not all letters will be as focused as the following example, but the elements remain the same.

If your letterhead does not contain it, include your name, title, and phone number. If handled effectively, the combination of direct mail and phone follow-up can generate a great deal of business.

Yet another benefit of the equipment you work with: You can generate all your direct-mail letters and merge them with your mailing list with various software programs. You will be amazed at how quickly and efficiently you can do work that would otherwise take hours, even days.

You may wonder why there are no price quotes on the sample direct-mail letter. Since each assignment will be different, according to what the customer requests, the charges will vary. It is important to be consistent, however. It might be a good idea to create a list of services and associated prices before the customers start to show up.

Here is a sample direct-mail letter to use as a springboard in writing your own:

Mary's Play House
123 Main Street, Anytown, USA • 123-4567

Dear Ms. Smith:

When you think about your most valued asset, what comes to mind? Your house? Car? Stocks and bonds?

How about your children? Is there really anything more valued to you than those youngsters? You look at them and think that you want only the best of everything for them. Nothing is too good for your kids.

Which is why they should only have the best childcare available. You and Mr. Smith can't be there 24 hours a day for the kids. Perhaps you both work and have a preschool-aged child who needs full-time care. Whatever your situation, you need a childcare resource that you can trust to provide loving and nurturing care to your precious little ones.

I'd like to introduce you to **Mary's Play House**, a new childcare service in your neighborhood. I started the service after doing a great deal of local research and talking with many families like yours. Based on the feedback, I have put together a program that will not only be thoroughly enjoyable for your children, but will also help them grow and learn.

Please come to Mary's Play House for a "Getting to Know You" evening on Friday, May 3rd. I'll provide refreshments, tell you about myself and my service, and show you what kind of care you can expect for your most valuable asset: your children.

Cordially,

Mary Soandso

Yellow Pages

Few successful businesspeople claim that they can build their businesses strictly by word-of-mouth referrals. A listing in the Yellow Pages is an absolute necessity if you're planning to build a full-scale operation.

Call the phone company and ask when the next directory is coming out. See what the deadline is for a Yellow Pages ad and plan accordingly. Buy the biggest ad you can afford. (You will be billed monthly by the phone company as part of your regular bill.) The cost of an ad can be as much as several hundred dollars per month, so buy your space carefully and ensure that it stands apart from the rest.

Plan ahead at least well enough to know what your business phone number will be, and try to open at about the same time that the new directory comes out.

Knowledge and belief in your product, faith in yourself, and respect for your customers are the keys to successfully building your future. As you go about starting and establishing your business, remember the word "profit." This alone should give you the necessary motivation to get out there and confidently tell the world what you have to offer.

Notes

Key Points

_____

_____

_____

_____

_____

_____

_____

Personal Thoughts

_____

_____

_____

_____

_____

_____

Additional Research

_____

_____

_____

_____

_____

_____

21

PROMOTION AND
PUBLIC RELATIONS

Informing the public about your business through the use of business cards, brochures, mailing pieces, catalogs, and specialty items (calendars, pens, and T-shirts imprinted with your company name) is a form of advertising that is known as promotion; what you do over and above your paid advertising and promotion that help build your image and keep your business in the public consciousness are referred to as public relations. There is a fine line between the two, and they can make or break your business if not addressed.

There are many clever ways to extend the effectiveness of your advertising and promotional dollars, as illustrated in the following examples.

A Little Creativity Goes a Long Way

The owner of a pet grooming business leaves a business card and a brochure featuring a 20 percent discount coupon everywhere he goes. When he is running errands, he always takes a handful of brochures with him to hand to store clerks, gas station attendants, and even foodservers he runs into during the day.

If he sees a car with a dog in it, or one with a bumper sticker announcing the owner's affection for a pet, he slips a brochure under the windshield wiper. Does it work? Absolutely. He claims that 45 percent of his new business comes from the recipients of his handouts, and the majority of them become regular customers.

Another business owner who operates a small walking tour service in her beachside town sends out a one-page quarterly newsletter featuring historical and other facts about the area to everyone who has ever taken the tour. She includes a $10 coupon that can be redeemed by former clients or their guests.

> *Advertisements contain the only truths to be relied on in a newspaper.*
>
> Thomas Jefferson

She states that many of her clients are local residents who send their out-of-town visitors on her walking tour, simply because she makes sure they are aware that she is still in business and generates enthusiasm through the newsletter.

Charity Tie-Ins

Other ideas you might consider include promoting humanitarian outreach. For example, for every ten products a customer buys or every tenth time a customer uses your service, you donate a predetermined amount of money to a local charity. You can easily keep track of customers' purchases by punching a hole at the edge of a card designed by you or your printer strictly for that purpose.

When you are ready to present the check to the particular charity, make sure the chairperson of the organization is there to accept it and be sure to contact the local press and invite them to the "event." In most cases, you'll receive free coverage.

According to successful entrepreneurs, free giveaways are the most successful promotions. You can order items such as pens, pencils, notepads, and calendars, just to name a few, with your name and phone number printed on them to give to people. Every time the recipient uses the item, he or she will automatically think of you! Check under "Advertising Specialties" in the Yellow Pages for prices and ideas.

Reminder Cards

Sending regular "thinking-of-you" cards to your past and present clientele is especially effective with service businesses. Again, it assures the client that you are friendly, reliable, and conscientious—real pluses for your credibility.

Networking

Check out local business-owner groups and the chamber of commerce in your area. Pay your membership dues and join as many groups as possible. Membership in these organizations offers you the opportunity to meet people who might use your service and will, at bare minimum, tell others about you once they know you, feel comfortable with you, and understand what you are offering. You will also be given a listing in the group's directory, generally under your specific category.

And, as is so often the case, members are prone to supporting others involved with their group. It is quite possible that members with compatible businesses will put a stack of your cards or brochures on their counter or in their referral file. In return, you may be able to promote their businesses to your customers. This is the true meaning of networking.

The directory also gives you bona-fide access to an instant mailing list, which you can use to send out promotional flyers or brochures. Participating in the organization's events and the willingness, for example, to speak at functions about your area of specialization will let people know that you are community-minded. This involvement will work to project a positive image for you and your business.

Customer Service

One of the most overlooked areas in promoting business is the way we create an impression when dealing with the public on a one-to-one basis. The ageless philosophy that the customer is always right and comes first has, it seems, gotten lost in the shuffle in these days of fast-paced transactions.

As a small business owner, you can be sure that customers will flock to you if you make them feel important. It is as easy as greeting them warmly (instruct your employees, if you have them, to do the same), maintaining a courteous attitude, and inviting them to come back soon.

Remember that word travels fast, and if you create an atmosphere that makes all your customers feel special, you can be sure they will tell their friends and neighbors.

Free Publicity

Free publicity also comes under the category of public relations. This includes newspaper, magazine, radio, and television interviews that feature interesting or unusual facts about you and your business.

As any newspaper reporter or talk-show host will tell you, everybody has a story to tell. The key is to get the media to zero in on yours and make it available to the public. If you have trouble deciding on a unique angle for your story, invite several friends over for a brainstorming session to create a newsworthy item.

Use your imagination to explore the creative possibilities of your business venture. And then look at your personal story. Perhaps you have completely switched fields with your new business: There's a story with a strong slant toward risk-taking. Maybe you have successfully turned a hobby into a business venture, created a unique product, or developed a new twist on an old theme. These all qualify as human-interest stories. Newspaper and magazine editors like them almost as much as their readers enjoy them.

Once you have your story angle, call the managing editor or the feature editor of your local newspaper. Give him or her a brief description of who you are and what business you are in.

Invite journalists to visit your place of business to get a firsthand look at what you are doing and how you do it. Do the same with program directors or talk-show hosts at local and regional television and radio stations.

If, on the first attempt, your presentation fails to result in an article, follow up in three to six months, possibly with a new story angle. In the meantime, however, send out regular press releases announcing new developments with your business—the grand opening, special events, details on your business philosophy, extra services, and features.

Even if they don't run a full story on you, there is a good possibility you could be included in a feature story about local entrepreneurs or people in related businesses.

An Effective Ad Campaign

All of the methods outlined earlier, along with any others you may develop, will keep your name in the consumer's mind. The effectiveness of an advertising and/or publicity campaign can be measured by conducting a simple marketing survey with new customers. Simply make it standard practice to ask each customer where he or she heard about you and your business.

Keep a tally of the responses in a notebook. A periodic review will give you hints of where to allocate future advertising funds. If, for example, the majority of your customers are being drawn from your display ad in the local newspaper, keep it going on a steady basis. The same principle applies to classified, direct-mail, or word-of-mouth advertising.

> *The advertisement is one of the most interesting and difficult of modern literary forms.*
>
> Aldous Huxley

The justification for investing in advertising and promotion is time. If you attempted to contact all of the people who read ads and press-release material in newspapers, or those who listen to talk shows, you would never have time to conduct your business.

Time is money! As a small business owner, you will want to devote as much attention as possible to the production end of your venture and let your advertising and promotion work bring in the customers.

Sample Press Release

FOR IMMEDIATE RELEASE

FOR MORE INFORMATION
Contact: Mary Soandso

Clown workshops, play acting, parades and art shows. Is this any way to run a childcare center?

"You bet!" says Mary Soandso, owner/operator of Mary's Play House at 123 Main Street in Anytown. "High quality, creative childcare is the most important issue facing parents in America today."

"As a result," she continued, "we are offering an innovative program that focuses on creative development and expression for children between the ages of six months and five years."

Ms. Soandso, a fifteen-year resident of Anytown, and her staff are committed to the concept of fun in educating the children of Anytown's working parents. Snacks are not just snacks, but an opportunity for kids to learn about measurements and colors by designing their own mid-day munchies. Even their infant charges are getting creative input through their involvement in parades around the playground and regular participation in events with the older toddlers.

An Open House will be held on Friday the 12th at 7:30 p.m. Parents are invited to bring their children for a hands-on tour of the center and an exciting new jungle gym in the playground. Refreshments will be served.

Mary's Play House is currently accepting applications for the fall season. Interested parents are invited to call 555-5555 to arrange an interview or to make reservations for the Open House.

Getting Started

At this point, you're ready to go out there and give the childcare business a try. If you've done your homework, by now you should know:

♦ What services you plan to provide

♦ What your prices will be for the services

♦ What your start-up costs and equipment needs are

♦ Some resources for equipment

♦ Where you will work—most likely home—and how to set up the space

♦ How to get started with advertising and promotion

It is absolutely crucial that you approach your start-up with good planning and organization. Take each step knowing what the previous step was and which step comes next. Likewise, know what you want to happen and what could happen; plan for problems, and have possible solutions ready.

As you review in your mind everything you've read here, remember this: While it's entirely possible to start a childcare business without much experience or training, you'll have a greater degree of success if you learn as much as you can, as fast as you can.

This book just scratches the surface of the knowledge that you will want—and need—to acquire in the course of starting your business and making it grow. There are many resources to help you learn and stay abreast of the industry's latest news. Some of these resources follow in the Appendix.

In closing, there are several points about you and your success in the childcare business that bear repeating:

1. The field of childcare is booming. With the right amount of effort and entrepreneurship, your ride on the wave can be quite comfortable.

2. Maintain a "customer-first" orientation. It will ensure repeat business and customer referrals.

3. Don't expect to succeed overnight. This can only serve to discourage you while things are slow.

Good luck to you in your new endeavor.

Notes

Personal Thoughts

Key Points

Additional Research

APPENDIX: RESOURCES

Associations and Agencies

Small Business Associations & Government Agencies

American Marketing Association
250 South Wacker Drive, Suite 200
Chicago, IL 60606-5819

Marketing publications available to nonmembers.

Bureau of the Census
Washington, DC 20233

Statistical data.

Chambers of Commerce
Consult Yellow Pages. Services vary among chambers but may
include advice, support, workshops or seminars, local business
news, and other services specifically for small businesses.

Council of Better Business Bureaus
4200 Wilson Boulevard, Suite 800
Arlington, VA 22203

Ask for a listing of their "Booklets on Wise Buying."

Dun & Bradstreet
299 Park Avenue
New York, NY 10171

Send for the booklet "This is Dun & Bradstreet," an overview of publications and services.

Internal Revenue Service (IRS)
1-800-829-1040 General tax assistance
1-800-829-3676 Forms and publications

See the government section of your phone book for address and phone of the local office. The IRS publishes a variety of books and brochures that are useful to owners of small businesses. Each year the IRS publishes "Tax Guide for Small Business."

International Franchise Association
1350 New York Avenue NW
Washington, DC 20005

Regulation and information on franchises.

Local Planning Agencies
See the government section of your phone book for address and phone of the local office. Source of information on zoning and future development locations.

Minority Business Development Agency
Office of Public Affairs
Department of Commerce
Washington, DC 20230

National Association for the Self-Employed
P.O. Box 612067
DFW Airport, TX 75261-2067

National Association of Women Business Owners
600 South Federal Street
Chicago, IL 60605

National Federation of Independent Business
150 West 20th Avenue
San Mateo, CA 94403

National Insurance Consumer Organization

P.O. Box 3243
Merrifield, VA 22116-3243

Send $3 and self-addressed, stamped #10 envelope for booklet, "Buyer's Guide to Insurance."

National Minority Business Council

235 East 42nd Street
New York, NY 10017

Bimonthly newsletter for small and minority businesses.

National Small Business United

1155 15th Street NW, Suite 710
Washington, DC 20005

Send for information on federal legislation.

Occupational Safety & Health Administration (OSHA)

Department of Labor
200 Constitution Avenue
Washington, DC 20210

Employment regulations.

Office of Information and Public Affairs

U.S. Department of Labor
200 Constitution Avenue NW
Washington, DC 20210

Request publications list regarding employment.

Service Corps of Retired Executives (SCORE)

See Small Business Administration.

Small Business Administration

1441 L Street NW
Washington, DC 20416

The SBA is the primary source of federal governmental assistance for small businesses. In addition to providing financing for many small businesses, it provides a number of services for free or at a small cost. SBA regional offices routinely conduct free or low-cost small business workshops. The SBA offers many helpful publications and the following hotlines:

SBA Answer Desk

Recorded information on a variety of topics.

1-800-827-5722

SBA Online

A bulletin board service that provides SBA information.

1-800-859-INFO if you use a 2400 baud modem or 800-697-INFO if you use a 9600 baud modem

Service Corps of Retired Executives (SCORE)

P.O. Box 15434
Fort Worth, TX 76119

Retired business executives offer their expertise and services to entrepreneurs through SBA's SCORE, which charges for out-of-pocket expenses but not for the consultant's time.

Telephone Company

Consult your local phone company. Most offer a variety of services and publications for small businesses.

AT&T 800-Number Information

Call 1-800 272-0400

Trade

Association of Child Care Consultants International

1801 Peachtree Street, Suite 160
Atlanta, GA 30309
(404) 352-8137

Association for Childhood Education International

3615 Wisconsin Avenue NW
Washington, DC 20016

Child Care America Inc.

14102 Warwick Boulevard
Newport News, VA 23602
(804) 886-0862

Child Care Information Exchange
P.O. Box 2890
Redmond, WA 98052
(301) 656-6666

Child Care Information Service
330 South Oak Knoll, Rm. 26
Pasadena, CA 91101
(818) 796-4341

Child Welfare League of America
67 Irving Place
New York, NY 10022

Child Care Law Center
625 Market Street, Suite 815
San Francisco, CA 94105
(415) 495-5498

National Association of Child Care Resource and Referral Agencies
2116 Campus Drive SE
Rochester, MN 55904
(507) 287-2220

National Association for Family Child Care
1331-A Pennsylvania Avenue NW, Suite 348
Washington, DC 20004
(800) 359-3817

National Association for the Education of Young Children
1834 Connecticut Avenue NW
Washington, DC 20009
(800) 424-2460

National Child Care Association
1029 Railroad Street
Conyers, GA 30207
(800) 543-7161

Non-Profit Child-Care Association
(800) 424-2460

Books

General Reference Books & Periodicals

Note: Many of the following resources are available through the Research Desk at your local library.

A Consumer's Guide to Telephone Service
Consumer Information Center, Pueblo, CO 81009

Bacon's Publicity Checker
A comprehensive listing of every major newspaper in the United States and Canada.

Encyclopedia of Associations
Published annually by Gale Research Company, Detroit, MI.

Financial Studies of the Small Business
Financial Research Associates
P.O. Box 7708
Winter Haven, FL 33883

National Five-Digit ZIP Directory (2 volumes)
U.S. Postal Service
6060 Primacy Parkway, Suite 101
Memphis, TN 38188-0001

Also available by phone 1-800-238-3150 or through your local post office.

Poor's Register of Corporations, Directors, and Executives
New York, NY: Standard & Poor's Corporation

Roget's Thesaurus in Dictionary Form
New York: HarperCollins, 1992

Synonyms and antonyms.

Tax Guide for Small Businesses

Internal Revenue Service publication. Published annually. Available from local IRS office.

Thomas Register of American Manufacturers

Thomas Publishing Company, New York, NY

Ulrich's International Periodicals Directory

Comprehensive listing of major magazines and newspapers.

Webster's New Collegiate Dictionary

Springfield, MA: G & C Merriam Company, 1989

Where to Find Business Information

by David Brownstone and Gorton Carruth

New York: John Wiley & Sons, 1982

Trade

A House Full of Kids: Running a Successful Day-Care Business in Your Home

by Karen Murphy

Boston: Beacon Press, 1984

The Infants We Care For

by L. Dittman

NAEYC
1834 Connecticut Avenue, NW
Washington, DC 20009

Quality Day Care: A Handbook of Choices of Parents and Caregivers

by R.C. Endsley and M.R. Bradbard

New Jersey: Prentice-Hall, 1981

Magazines and Publications

General Business

Entrepreneur Magazine
2392 Morse Avenue
Irvine, CA 92714

Published monthly.

Sales & Marketing Management
Bill Communications, Inc.
355 Park Avenue South
New York, NY 10010

Published monthly except in June, August, and October, when it is published twice a month.

Working Woman
Lang Communications
230 Park Avenue, 7th Floor
New York, NY 10169

Published monthly.

Trade

Beginnings
P.O. Box 2890
Redmond, WA 98073

Day Care and Early Childhood Education
92 Fifth Avenue
New York, NY 10011

Parents Magazine
Parents Institute
Bergenfield, NJ 07621

Working Parents
Box 279
Bronxville, NY 10708

INDEX

P

Parents
feedback from, 34-35
interviewing, 92
responsibilities of, 25-26
Partnerships, 118, 119
considering, 141
Part-time start-up, 140-141
Patience, as an entrepreneurial
trait, 10, 12
Payment policy, 176
Pension programs, 112
People, working with, 10
Periodicals, 230-232
Peripherals, 46
Permits, 117-118
Perseverance, as an en-
trepreneurial trait, 10, 14
Personal activities, allotting time
for, 98
Personal balance sheet, 162
Personality, financial, 68
Personality traits, 9-14
"Personalized care," pricing for,
174
Personal loans, 150
Personnel management, 195
Philosophy, statement of, 26
Phone calls, limiting, 187-188
Physical count inventory control,
181
Pick-up/drop-off service, 92
Planning, 3-4, 5. See also
Business plan
importance of, 131
of time, 188
Play areas, 93

Play equipment, 41
Positive reinforcement, 187
Positive thinking, 12
in approaching lenders, 148
Potential Clients and Contacts
List, 78
Preparedness, 3-4
Preplanning, 35-36, 77
Press release, sample, 222
Pricing, 165-177. See also Profit
of childcare, 172-176
considerations for, 174-176
fair, 167
guidelines for, 165-167
Pricing formula, 167
Printer covers, 51
Printers, computer, 48-49
Printing, costs of, 71
Problems list, 26
Procrastination, 187
Product-location match, 104
Product-market match, 83
Products, pricing, 166
Professional discounts, 42
Professional fees, 71
Professional services, 109-112
Profit, 153
calculating, 170
inventory and, 180
potential for, xiii-xiv, 20,
22-23
pricing and, 165-177
Profit-loss projections, 144
Progress review, 88, 107
Projected Expense Statement, 67,
69, 74
Projected Income Statement, 70

BUSINESS REPLY MAIL

FIRST CLASS MAIL   PERMIT NO. 11201   SAN DIEGO, CA

POSTAGE WILL BE PAID BY ADDRESSEE

PFEIFFER & COMPANY

8517 PRODUCTION AVE

SAN DIEGO, CA 92121-9645

NO POSTAGE
NECESSARY
IF MAILED
IN THE
UNITED STATES

BUSINESS REPLY MAIL

FIRST CLASS MAIL   PERMIT NO. 11201   SAN DIEGO, CA

POSTAGE WILL BE PAID BY ADDRESSEE

PFEIFFER & COMPANY

8517 PRODUCTION AVE

SAN DIEGO, CA 92121-9645

Get a FREE catalogue of
performance-boosting resources!

Pfeiffer
& COMPANY
INTERNATIONAL PUBLISHERS

□ **YES!** Please send me your current catalogue with your complete collection of human resource development materials.

Name _____

Job Title _____

Organization _____

Mailing Address _____

City/Town _____

State/Prov./District _____

Postal/Zip Code _____ Country/County_____

Internet E-mail Address_____

Phone_____ Fax _____

Don't forget your colleagues! *Please give this card to (or complete for) a friend if you already receive the Pfeiffer & Company catalogue.*

Get a FREE catalogue of
performance-boosting resources!

Pfeiffer
& COMPANY
INTERNATIONAL PUBLISHERS

□ **YES!** Please send me your current catalogue with your complete collection of human resource development materials.

Name _____

Job Title _____

Organization _____

Mailing Address _____

City/Town _____

State/Prov./District _____

Postal/Zip Code _____ Country/County_____

Internet E-mail Address_____

Phone_____ Fax _____

Don't forget your colleagues! *Please give this card to (or complete for) a friend if you already receive the Pfeiffer & Company catalogue.*